KT-233-959

POWER PLAYS
PRIMARY SCHOOL CHILDREN'S CONSTRUCTIONS OF GENDER, POWER, AND ADULT WORK

c.

WITHDRAWN FROM
THE LIBRARY

UNIVERSITY OF
WINCHESTER

KA 0244964 1

POWER PLAYS
PRIMARY SCHOOL CHILDREN'S CONSTRUCTIONS OF GENDER, POWER, AND ADULT WORK

Becky Francis

Trentham Books

First published in 1998 by Trentham Books Limited

Trentham Books Limited
Westview House
734 London Road
Oakhill
Stoke on Trent
Staffordshire
England ST4 5NP

© Becky Francis 1998

All rights reserved. No part of this publication may be reproduced in any material form (including photocopying or storing it in any medium by electronic means and whether or not transiently or incidentally to some other use of this publication) without the prior written permission of the copyright owner, except in accordance with the provision of the Copyright, Designs and Patents Act 1988 or under the terms of a licence issued by the Copyright Licensing Agency, 90 Tottenham Court Road, London W1P 9HE. Applications for the Copyright owner's written permission to reproduce any part of this publication should be addressed in the first instance to the publisher.

British Cataloguing in Publication Data
A catalogue record for this book is available from the British Library

ISBN 1 85856 097 7
(hb ISBN 1 85856 113 2)

Cover illustration by Peter Francis

KING ALFRED'S COLLEGE
WINCHESTER

0244964 | 155·424
FRA

Designed and typeset by Trentham Print Design Ltd., Chester and printed in Great Britain by Design 2 Print, Llandudno, North Wales.

CONTENTS

Acknowledgements

There are many people who have played a part in the creation of this book.

This work would not have been possible without the good-humoured co-operation of the staff and pupils at the schools in which I conducted research and I want to thank them for their help and patience. I'm particularly grateful to the children, who were so friendly and open with me and such good fun.

The book is based on my PhD, and the advice and support of my supervisors Merryn Hutchings and Sue Lees were invaluable to its successful completion. Elizabeth Wilson and Alistair Ross both contributed by reading and commenting on my work. I should also like to thank Gillian Klein and Trentham Books for taking on this publication, as book proposals based on PhD theses tend to be viewed warily by publishers. During my time as a PhD student at University of North London my colleagues Vanda Corrigan and Cass Mitchell-Riddell helped me greatly with humour and feedback, and gave much-needed reminders that there is life beyond your PhD! At the University of Greenwich Patrick Ainley and Diana Jones encouraged me to write the book, and I also thank Jocelyn Robson and Merryn Hutchings (UNL) for their advice on it. Thanks too to Salim Nazeer for helping me with suggestions for the children's pseudonyms.

Some of the data discussed in this book has been presented in journal articles. My thanks to the editors of *Gender and Education, British Journal of Sociology of Education, British Journal of Education and Work; Educational Research, Children's Social and Economics Education*, and *Journal of Applied Psychology* for allowing me to reproduce material here.

I thank my family, particularly Diana, Nico, Cath, Lisa, my grandparents, and my Lam nieces, for their continual support and interest in my work. Especial thanks to Peter Francis for his cover cartoon. My friends Angela Robinson, Suzanne Hudson, Caron Elgey and Katherine Srodzinski have all been great – the latter would not claim interest in my work, but has still provided light relief! And finally I thank my partner Daniel Hew, for being great.

CHAPTER 1

INTRODUCTION

Society remains strongly gender-differentiated, and this book sets out to find out why. The data and research are drawn from my PhD research in primary schools. It is feminist research, motivated by a wish to contribute to understanding of the gendered nature of society so that we can change things. There are many different types of feminist. Liberal feminists work for equal opportunity between the sexes, and some radical feminists believe that although the genders are different, women's experience is at least as positive as men's. *My* feminist position is not simply that both genders should have equal opportunity, or that the genders are different, but that gender is cultural. During my research, many children were keen to point out to me that 'men can't have babies'. True – but I feel that the biology assigned to one at birth has little connection to the gendered positions and attitudes we take up in our lives. These gendered positions vary enormously between cultures but in the vast majority it is the attributes denoted as *feminine* which are attributed less value in that society.

Gendered society

Despite recent social changes, society remains gender differentiated, and women remain disadvantaged. Over the last twenty years in Britain, females have been gradually catching up with males in terms of educational achievement. They are now matching males in exam success in the majority of subjects, right up to university entrance level[1]. Women are now as successful as men at degree level (though the genders remain fairly polarised in terms of degree subject, and more men achieve First Class Honours degrees). Simultaneously over the

1

past decade the proportion of women in paid employment has increased. A growing number of women are working outside the home: over half have paid jobs, though only a quarter of these are full time.

Yet a number of studies have shown that despite this increase in the number of women engaging in paid work, they still earn less than men, and still do the vast majority of housework in addition to their paid jobs (see, for instance, Central Statistical Office, 1995; Arnot, 1997). Although women's increasing success in education may be too recent a development to have made a significant impact on their career success, these studies show that women's gradually improved educational success has not *yet* lead to an increase in the number of women gaining top managerial, governmental and professional posts. Nor has the greater number of women in the British workplace had an impact on 'feminising' that environment: much gender discrimination persists in policy and practice (Cockburn, 1987, 1991; Stafford, 1991). Research has shown that sexual harassment is still frequent (see Pattinson, 1991). Childcare facilities remain few and far between, and maternity leave is generally portrayed as a privilege. Taking time off to have or care for children can mean sacrificing career progression, as part-time work or career-gaps are viewed by employers as incompatible with ambition and promotion. Moreover, paternity leave remains tokenistic, if available at all (Connell, 1995), which means that men are deprived of taking an equal part in bringing up their children. Moreover, it perpetuates the assumption that it is women who should take career-breaks on behalf of their children's care; even if they earn more than their partners, or the father would prefer to be responsible for childcare. The issue is not just which gender performs paid work or non-paid caring/ housework but the different values our society ascribes to these gendered occupations. It is assumed that men should take the main responsibility for paid work – they are, after all, more competitive, brave and ambitious than women. Whereas caring for children is primarily women's task – they are softer, more emotional. Caring for children and the family is not even considered 'proper' work.

So society remains gender-differentiated. According to the mass media, we live in a 'post-feminist' society – the implication being that feminism, while a rather extreme and naively radical movement, did have a part to play in working towards a fairer society, but that now gender equality has been realised, those awful feminists can be safely consigned to history. Academic and media attention is now being focused on the supposedly contemporary issue of boys' educational 'disadvantage'. As Yates (1997) argues, discussion of this kind usually assumes that because of an emphasis on improving educational opportunities for girls over the last twenty years, girls have achieved educational success at the expense of boys. In fact, as Weiner *et al* (1997) argue, girls have been doing well at exams (except in the most 'masculine' subjects) for a long time: it is simply the current exam-focused educational culture which is drawing attention to it. I recently attended an educational research conference where some academics appeared to be suggesting that the failure of many boys, and rising exclusion rates for boys in primary and secondary school, indicated that we should return to the old ways of learning where boys seemed to do better. The fact that girls constitute more than half the pupil population, and are apparently performing better under current conditions, did not appear to deter this idea!

I have some of my own suggestions about boys' educational achievement, drawn from my research findings, which I will return to in the final chapter. This aside, it is certainly true that, as Weiner *et al* (1997) observe, great gains have been made by the liberal feminist movement in terms of equality of opportunity. However, as I argued above, the glass ceiling remains firmly in place because the assumptions about gender difference, gendered roles and characteristics, and the ways in which those characteristics are evaluated by society, have not altered. Despite equal opportunities legislation, and much institutional rhetoric concerning equality, the sex we are assigned still has a massive impact on the shape of our lives and on our perceptions of ourselves. This book examines possible explanations for this situation and discusses what might be done to alter it.

Before I discuss the findings and implications of my research in school in the following chapters, I will explain the theoretical framework for my research on gender differentiation. This discussion deals with post-structuralist/post-modern approaches – terms which some readers may respond to with an inward groan because they are so often used with little explanation but much confusing jargon. Such theoretical approaches often deter educationalists as they offer so little suggestion for translation into practice. One of the main claims of post-structuralist and post-modern approaches is that they deconstruct dominant or traditional 'discourses' and assumptions of society. However, they often do this in exclusive, over-complicated language which excludes the majority of readers, thus perpetuating modes of academic/intellectual superiority and exclusivity in a far from radical way! The post-structuralist writer in the social sciences, Michel Foucault, appears a prime example. He rattles on in a self-assured, authoritarian voice, often using Latin without translation. He frequently refers to sources as diverse as the Marquis de Sade, Neitzsche, and ancient theologians without any explanation, as though he assumes the reader is as familiar with their works as he is[2]. This may inspire awe in the reader but does not aid clarity. As a feminist I think it important that research should be accessible and practical (see Stanley and Wise, 1993). Post-structuralist and post-modernist theories offer some exciting and radical ideas which should be of wide interest but if they cannot be articulated in a relatively accessible way they will have little impact. Therefore my discussion of these theoretical positions will be as straightforward as possible, and where I resort to jargon, I shall try to clarify my meaning.

I begin by discussing the short-comings of 'social-learning' theories which attempted to explain the reproduction of gender roles in our society. I then explain the bases of post-structuralist theory, and analyse the arguments for and against the use of post-structuralist theory in research on gender. This issue has been widely debated[3], but it is has not yet been moved forward. Having argued that 'pure' post-structuralism is incompatible with the feminist emancipatory project, I suggest that 'pure' post-structuralism may be something of a fallacy; and certainly not practicable in educational research. Instead, a new combination of feminist and post-structuralist theories is put forward that combines the beneficial elements of post-structuralist theory with a feminist approach.

Social Learning Theory

Since the nineteenth century, schooling has been singled out by feminists as a strong influence on the perpetuation of traditional gender roles. Social learning, or 'sex role' theory appealed to many feminists in the 1970s and '80s because it offers a purely social (non-biological) account of the gendered nature of society. Women's lack of power in society was attributed by many feminists to a process of socialisation that begins in the family and is reinforced in schools. Thus it was argued that girls failed in educational settings because of a 'hidden curriculum' of taught sex-roles and assumptions about the comparative inferiority of girls. Feminist researchers such as Sue Sharpe (1976), Dale Spender (1982) and Michelle Stanworth (1981) showed how teachers devoted less attention and time to girls, and held low (if any) career expectations for them. They explained how boys dominated the classroom physically and verbally and how they belittled the girls and their gender. They also identified the male domination of school policy and curriculum design, showing how 'feminine' subjects are devalued, and female experience and contributions ignored or trivialised in history, literature, etc. These and other studies made a convincing argument and highlighted the disadvantages and trials most girls faced in the classroom. They maintained that a self-fulfilling prophecy was in operation, whereby girls' confidence was undermined by their schooling experience. Because their expectations were thus lowered, girls did not prioritise exam and career success but saw their future primarily in terms of being wives and mothers (for which they needed no academic qualifications). In this way, gender roles were perpetuated.

However, flaws in this 'reproduction of roles' idea gradually became evident. In his influential study of working-class groups of boys at a secondary school, Willis (1977) showed that boys did not simply take up roles in any passive or uniform way but actively constructed their own positions, often resisting the guidance offered by the school. The concept of resistance, and the issue of change in social relationships over time, cannot be explained by social learning theories, because such accounts see fixed roles being reproduced continually by the 'agents of socialisation' (education, the family, mass-media, etc). Many feminist studies have addressed this issue, arguing, for example, that girls take up gender roles in multiple and contradictory ways, simultaneously accommodating and resisting them. Davies (1989) also points out that people are not simply passive recipients of socialisation but that they actively construct and impact upon the world, thus shaping their own lives and the lives of others.

Moreover, the fact that women have attained far greater educational success over the last twenty years and that more than half of all British women now engage in paid work, illustrate two recent social changes which cannot be explained by socialisation theories of role repro-duction. Despite their apparently continuing marginalisation in the classroom, girls are now on average as successful as boys in terms of exam achievement and may even be performing slightly better overall. So girls are apparently performing better than they used to *despite* continuing discrimination and harassment on the part of male students and staff (which feminists previously postulated as explaining girls' comparative failure in the education system). Connell (1987, 1995) concludes therefore that socialisation and sex role theories founder because they cannot account for such changes in gender relations.

Consequently many feminist researchers (myself included), sought new and more flexible explanations of the gendered nature of society, and some have turned to post-structuralist theory. The terms 'post-structuralism' and post-modernism' are sometimes confused and occasionally appear to be used synonymously. 'Post-modernism' refers to a body of work which revels in the recent fragmentation of modernist narratives and claims to scientific truth. Its foremost ex-ponent is Lyotard (1984). Post-structuralism, on the other hand, refers specifically to the structuralist movement in literary criticism. Structuralists argued that all human narratives are based on similar known story-lines and that because words (or 'signifiers') structure our thoughts we are trapped a 'prison-house of language' (see Sassure, 1916). A universal social order is constructed through language – notions of ourselves as autonomous individuals are simply discourses within which human lives are positioned. Post-structuralists such as Derrida (1976) and Barthes (1990) take issue with this interpretation, arguing that language can be interpreted in many different ways and that dominant storylines or claims to truth can be 'deconstructed' and dismantled. In the social sciences, Foucault (1972) shows how ideas assumed to have always been present in society are actually historically and culturally specific, and have developed and altered, or been replaced, at different times in history.

The benefits of post-structuralist theory

Many recent feminist studies have used the post-structuralist theory of *discursive positioning* as an analytical tool in their investigations. Foucault (1980) argues that personality is not fixed: instead people are positioned and position others in 'discourse' – socially and culturally produced patterns of language. Power is embedded in discourses, because of their ability to construct people in particular ways. A housewife, for example, could be positioned as fulfilling her natural role through traditionalist discourses of gender essentialism, or could be positioned as a victim of oppression in feminist discourse. This theory offers an explanation which can incorporate the notions of resistance and contradiction which proved so problematic for sex-role theory. People are passively positioned in certain discourse but are at the same time active in *positioning* in other discourse. According to Foucault (1980), wherever there is discourse there is resistance: for instance, if a person is positioned as powerless by one discourse, s/he may position her/himself as powerful via an alternative discourse.

This post-structuralist theory of power positioning offers an explanation for other theoretical complexities that have challenged feminism: for example, the ways in which power is wielded between women (and between men), as well as between men and women. Black, working class, gay, and disabled feminists have drawn white, middle-class, able-bodied, heterosexual feminists' attention to the fact that oppressive power relationships are not dependent *only* on gender but also on a host of other factors, and can exist between women. Foucault maintains that power is not a possession but is constituted through multiple and constantly shifting discourses. He describes power as:

> never localised here or there, never in anybody's hands, never appropriated as commodity or a piece of wealth. Power is exercised through a net-like organisation. And not only do individuals circulate between its threads; they are always in the position of simultaneously undergoing and exercising this power. They are not only its inert or consenting target; they are always also the elements of its articulation. (1980, p.98)

Thus we might, for instance, be rendered powerless by gender discourse in one instance, while positioning ourselves (or being positioned) as powerful via social class discourse in another. Jones (1997) takes issue with some post-structuralist-feminist assumptions that people can actively choose to position themselves as powerful by drawing on certain discourses. While I would maintain that this *does* occasionally happen (and hope to illustrate this in my data chapters), often this positioning of others or oneself is subconscious. However, it is a perpetual aspect of human interaction.

Foucault's work also shares the feminist criticism of 'enlightenment'[4] discourses and constructs. Enlightenment discourses take a scientific approach to the world, implying a possible analytical objectivity, and a separating off of the reasoning mind (constructed as male) from the emotions and body (constructed as female). Foucault reveals enlightenment discourse to be socially constructed, an argument also made by many feminists[5].

The repudiation of the notion of a static identity means that gender is not fixed but rather that people are positioned in gender discourse. This challenges gender essentialism. Radical and *difference* feminists see 'womanhood' as an homogeneous group, arguing that an 'essential feminine' exists. However, these notions have appeared self-subverting to many other feminists, as they effectively explain, and therefore in a sense legitimise, the difference between women's and men's social power. Post-structuralist theory enables us to argue that there is no essential 'femaleness'. Instead, dominant discourses of gender position all people as male or female, and provide narratives about the ways in which those people should behave and what they should desire. Following from this, some feminists argue that the terms 'woman' and 'girl' may be misleading and redundant, as they imply a fixity and homogeneity which do not exist.

The idea that gender is not fixed but rather that we are positioned and position ourselves in gender discourse has been interpreted as encouraging by some feminists. For instance, Davies (1989) argues that the analysis of gender discourse will provide us with a new understanding of the way in which we are positioned within that discourse. She and others maintain that this raises the possibility of our creating *new* gender discourses, and thus re-shaping ourselves and our lives through discourse.

Feminist research using a post-structuralist approach

Certainly, post-structuralism has been put to good use in some feminist educational research. Valerie Walkerdine has used post-structuralist discourse analysis extensively in her work, particularly exploring the ways that different discourses can position girls and women. Drawing on Foucault's (1972, 1977, 1981) approach in locating and investigating discourses in history, Walkerdine (1988) has shown how girls are seen to 'fail' at maths because of their positioning in various, historically specific, discourses. She argues that educational, child-centred discourses (born of the popularisation of Piagetian approaches to education of the 1960s) delineate a 'right way' of learning maths, based on ideas of play and experimentation. These replaced previously dominant discourses of rote learning which stressed diligence and practice rather than play. Thus boys' experimentation with maths is positioned through child-centred discourses as 'the correct way' to learn maths, whereas girls' more diligent approach is associated with conformity and rote learning, and is positioned as repressive and erroneous (although these educational discourses may be changing again in recent years, as I discuss in the final chapter). Walkerdine also examines how liberal-democratic and child-centred discourses position mothers and teachers as facilitators to the development of 'the child', and working-class approaches to parenting as erroneous and repressive.

In a similar way to Walkerdine, Bronwyn Davies (1989, 1993) used a post-structuralist analysis for her research in the pre-school and primary school. Davies' original research was motivated by a concern to discover why, despite anti-sexist parenting, children often still appear to take up gender in stereotypical ways. She had also noticed that when she read what she had interpreted as an anti-sexist fairy tale to a young female listener, the child did not interpret or 'hear' the story in the same way that Davies did. So she decided to investigate the processes through which pre-school children are constituted as either male or female. She concludes from her findings that gender discourse presents the social world as split into a clear, relational dichotomy of male/female duality. Children construct the taking up of these relational gendered positions as vital for social competence and identity. The depiction of gender identity is a public achievement: therefore, Davies argues, children take up aspects of gender-stereotypical behaviour in order to publicly delineate their gender identification. A child who does not conform to gender norms of behaviour may be marginalised and viewed as 'not a real person', and because one gender is only recognised in relation to the other, such a child also challenges the gender identities of other children by throwing the gender dichotomy into doubt. Thus in order to protect their identities children participate in 'gender category maintenance work': this involves the taking up of a gender position with outward shows of stereotypical masculinity or femininity and coercing their peers to do the same, in an attempt to create a firmer gender identity. Thus gender is collectively constructed and maintained.

According to Davies, children and adults have access to different discourses: though we all draw on the dominant discourse of a dualistic gender dichotomy, gender maintenance and discourses pertaining to child behaviour – e.g. 'naughtiness', 'messiness', etc. – are more salient to children, whereas other discourses may be more salient to adults. This, she claimed, was the reason why feminist stories were not 'heard' by children in the same way as adults. Davies found that the ways in which children took up gender were multiple, complex and contradictory, and that the gender dichotomy was resisted by some children. This finding supports her post-structuralist argument that if children can refuse certain discursive practices, it may be possible to resist the dominant discourse of gender duality by creating new forms of discourse, allowing new gender positionings.

Thus Davies' findings go some way towards explaining the persistently gendered nature of society: she argues that children do not take up gender positions because of some inherent urge but because of dominant discursive practices which position us all as either male or female, as though the two are relational categories.

Difficulties with the combination of feminism and post-structuralism

Despite the apparent benefits of post-structuralist approaches for feminism, there appear to be two fundamental conflicts between feminist and post-structuralist theory which make them incompatible. The first is the clash between modernist (feminist) and post-structura-

list positions; and the second is the post-structuralist aim of deconstruction compared to the feminist need for a system to explain the
socio-economic reality of gender difference.

I sought to investigate the various constructions and power positions
formed through gender discourse: this is based on a post-structuralist
perspective. But I also intended to analyse the *impact* of gender discourses on people's constructions of power and further the understanding of these discursive processes, so that we have a better chance
of changing them. This is based on my feminist intentions. Thus my
research has emancipatory aims. Yet such political, emancipatory concerns are dismissed by post-structuralists as repressive discourses –
'modernist truth narratives' – which should themselves be deconstructed rather than developed. Feminism is an inherently modernist
theory in that it supposes a founding subject ('womanhood'); and is
based on the 'truth narrative' that patriarchy oppresses women, and the
moral assumption that such oppression is wrong and that we should
work to end this oppression (see Balbus, 1987). Hence feminism is an
enlightenment project, born of the humanist, enlightenment idea that
the world can be made a better place through human endeavour (Soper,
1990). To post-structuralists, 'truth discourses' or 'grand narratives'
exercise a power relationship, as they claim truths or moral correctness
and involve totalitarian generalisations. The work of many post-structuralist authors aims to reveal how these claims to moral truth are built
on subjective cultural discourses, by deconstructing these narratives.

This deconstruction could also be applied to much non-feminist educational research. The majority of educational research concerned, for
instance, with teaching practice, is framed within an enlightenment supposition that education is basically positive (even potentially emancipatory), and that educational methods, policy and practice can and
should be improved for the benefit of students and society as a whole.
This educational discourse constitutes another liberal grand narrative.

I observed that many feminists have perceived the idea of the post-
structuralist deconstruction of gender as a liberating one. However,
others have observed that 'womanhood' is indispensable to feminism:
it is the very basis of feminist thought, and without it there would be
no feminism. Moreover, this concern over the deconstruction or reten-

tion of the category 'woman' ties in with another feminist criticism of post-structuralism: the suggestion that the theory is divorced from social reality. For example, feminist philosopher Kate Soper (1990) notes post-structuralist Jacques Derrida's (1976) argument that we should abandon the category 'woman' in order to break down the gender dichotomy. Soper observes that not only is Derrida's argument self-subverting (in that he must allude to the category 'woman' in order to urge us to abandon it), but also that Derrida shows a lack of understanding about social reality. She argues that gender discourses have a very real impact on our lives: a woman may still fear a man when walking alone at night, whether or not she agrees theoretically that we should reject the categories 'male' and 'female'. Similarly, Lloyd and Duveen (1992) argue that post-structuralist analysis does not recognise how gender positions constrain certain types of interaction. 'Power' is used by Foucault in a very general sense, and Foucauldian theory has still not provided an adequate explanation of the nature and source of power and how it is exercised against women (see Soper, 1993a).

Feminist research is motivated by emancipatory aims. Because of its rejection of structured narratives and truth discourses, post-structuralism is, according to many feminists, unable to engage in theorising, or work for, social change. This post-structuralist focus on deconstruction rather than construction can result in political nihilism and fatalism. As Squires (1993) puts it, post-structuralism deconstructs all 'principled positions' (ethical evaluations), thus causing political and ethical paralysis. Without grand narratives it becomes impossible to generalise about power relations. Accordingly, Maynard (1994) concludes that post-structuralist theory renders social research pointless.

Maynard questions the relevance of a theory which deconstructs other theories but appears to provide nothing to replace them with. This tendency of post-structuralism has been conceded by Foucault: Ramazanoglu (1993) reports Foucault's acknowledgement of the gap between his own liberal impulses and the conservative implications of his theory which removes the grounds for political action. Other writers argue that, more than simply failing to help feminism, post-structuralism is an androcentric, even reactionary theory. Cole and Hill (1995) argue that post-modernism reveals its reactionary tendencies in its rejection of emancipatory narratives, and that it consequently disempowers the oppressed, and upholds the Radical Right. Bordo (1990) and Hartsock (1990) suggest that post-structuralism is a reactionary male ploy to undermine the gains of feminist theory. Hartsock asks:

> Why is it that just at the moment when so many of us who have been silenced begin to demand the right to name ourselves, to act as subjects rather than objects of history, that just then the concept of subjecthood becomes problematic? Just when we are forming our own theories of the world, uncertainty emerges about whether the world can be theorised. (1990, p.163)

Thus Hartsock builds on Balbus' (1987) argument that post-structuralist theory deprives feminists of the conceptual tools they had developed to explain and combat their subordination.

Attempts to circumvent the conflicts between feminism and post-structuralism

Some pro-post-structuralist feminists have tried to circumvent these apparent incompatibilities. For example, Fraser and Nicholson (1990) and Weedon (1987) argue that it is acceptable to continue with the feminist grand narrative intact, so long as feminists acknowledge the 'historicity' of their theories. However, this appears unacceptably apologetic: like Spretnak (1993), I suggest that feminists and other researchers should be proud of their emancipatory aims and beliefs and note that this emancipatory narrative is the basis of most feminist research.

Davies (1989, 1993) argues that because of her post-structuralist perspective she no longer has to worry about the contradictions or inconsistencies between the different theories she utilises; post-structuralist theory reveals the impossibility of coherence and unity. While I agree that we all think and behave in multiple and contradictory ways[6], and that we should recognise this in our work, I argue that Davies' position is unsatisfactory for two main reasons. Firstly, the acceptance of total incoherence and contradiction could endorse the use of reactionary discourse or fragment the feminist narrative altogether. And secondly, the avocation of such an incoherent approach raises important questions about the status of research work. While it may be radical to suggest that research work and subsequent publications are no more credible or privileged than any other sort of writing, in this case there is no reason why anyone should bother *reading* such publications, let alone consider or carry out their suggestions. The deconstruction of the 'will to truth' in academic research is a concept itself worthy of further consideration and research.

So my problems with post-structuralism remain. However, most post-structuralist-feminists have in fact retained the categories 'men' and 'women' (or 'boys' and 'girls') in their research, and have stated their feminist – thus modernist and emancipatory – approach. I would argue that this is not a fully post-structuralist position. However, realising this made me look again at post-structuralism.

Questioning post-structuralism and adding feeling

At what point does an idea become a theory and a theory become a narrative/discourse? Is not post-structuralism itself a narrative of sorts? Although truth discourses present a narrative search for order and 'truth', discourses which preach *disorder* and deconstruction are also narratives, albeit subversive ones. Despite the absence of belief in a 'founding subject' they are still based on a theory or position about the world (the theory that there is no coherent personhood and that there can be no modernist certainty or truth), and they postulate an ideal or method to follow (deconstruction of truth narratives). Balbus (1987) supports this interpretation, maintaining that even in Foucault's writings there appears a 'latent discourse' where the evils of 'continuous history' and 'totality' retain a prominent place, and where the argument that history consists of a succession of power/knowledge discourses itself constitutes a claim to Truth.

The structuring of our experience in the form of narratives is, according to Sarbin (1986) universal throughout human culture. He argues that the formation of explanatory and structuring narratives is an inherent part of being human. Therefore narratives may be present in post-structuralist works as well as in modernist theory, despite denial, since theorists from both perspectives hold their humanity in common.

Spretnak (1993) scathingly observes that many academics self-consciously attempt not to make 'truth claims', or even appear hopeful about social change, in their attempts to appear 'post-structurally correct'. She claims that people who were motivated by egalitarian concerns to change the world have been rendered impotent by the nihilistic tendencies of post-modern theory, which denies the validity of emancipatory projects. Spretnak implies that these writers still *feel* that we should act on the world, but cannot harmonise this feeling with their cynical post-modern theories. This view is supported by Connor (1993), who argues that issues of value have not disappeared in post-structuralist work but have simply been hidden. Billig (1987, 1988) argues that all ideology and argument is dilemmatic: for every argument we articulate we are aware of a contrary, counter-argument, which is also a part of our construction. I too feel that this is a useful analysis of our thought processes and use of discourse. However, the word *feel* is stressed, because (as Billig's theory implies) at the same time as I articulate my support for this position I am aware of a counter-argument that suggests thought is unitary. I feel that Billig's explanation is a better argument than the counter-argument. The point is that, as Billig's argument suggests, there can still be one side of arguments which we agree with or feel to be 'true', despite our acceptance that we have other discourses to draw on.

Middleton (1992) agrees that in all human conduct we are constantly making value judgements and argues that these evaluations are often based on feeling and impulse. He suggests that many male academics, including post-structuralists, suffer from the male fear of feeling (impulse) and emotion, based on the idea of the separation between the reasoning mind (male) and the emotional body (female). By 'giving way' to impulsive feeling, the reasoning mind can no longer be separated from the (uncivilised) body. Yet, Middleton argues, feeling and emotion do count in our thoughts and expressions. Thus to deny our feelings and preferences (which form, and give preference to, narratives), is to maintain a falsehood and to deny subjectivity (Abrams, 1996). As Rose (1989) argues, we have to recognise our socially produced modernity.

I conclude, then, that while we may agree theoretically that people are positioned and position through discourse, we still *feel* ourselves to have agency, moral obligation and preferences for different kinds of discourse. Also, creating narratives to structure or describe our lives is part of being human. This position, which can combine a theoretical post-structuralism with an acknowledgement that we still *feel* ourselves to be active, choice-making human agents, is far more compatible with a feminist perspective. Thus I still *feel* that the feminist argument is valid, despite my recognition that it is a modernist grand narrative, based on (probably over-) essentialist generalisations concerning 'males' and 'females'. Soper (1990) argues that although feminism should move towards indifference feminism and away from *difference* (essentialist) feminism, the category 'woman' should be retained as a tool to describe and transform women's lives in order to bring us to a position where we can afford to be gender-indifferent. Bailey (1993) supports this view, calling it 'strategic essentialism'.

Similarly Harding (1990, 1991) argues that enlightenment discourses have progressive as well as regressive tendencies, and that we need post-structuralist *and* enlightenment agendas at this time in history. These arguments advocate a kind of 'post-modern-modern', or 'post-post-structuralism', in which feminists can combine post-modern theories and aims with a humanist approach as a method of reaching a position where we can realise post-structuralist aims. Balbus (1987) maintains that we can (and should) distinguish between libertarian and authoritarian truth discourses, and that feminism is a libertarian discourse. This involves a value judgement but, as I have argued, making value judgements is part of being human. Hence in this book I draw upon the parts of post-structuralism which I *feel* are useful for feminism. This is certainly a 'post-modern modern' position, but I recognise the inconsistencies in it and claim that they are a part of the dilemmatic human condition (see Billig, 1987, 1988).

Deconstruction of gender

The aim of deconstruction of the gender dichotomy, supported by myself and Davies, warrants some discussion. Soper (1990, 1993b) has questioned the desirability of a 'genderless utopia', arguing that feminists' allusions to such a society appear very vague. Certainly, while gender essentialism of *difference* feminists has been criticised by many others as over-stereotyped and restrictive, relatively few feminists have declared themselves in favour of the total deconstruction of the gender dichotomy[7]. A 'genderless society' may have limited appeal, when much of our sense of identity is derived from our gender. Many feminists have celebrated women's difference from men, focusing on the benefits of being female and the negativity of masculinity. This lack of commitment to the deconstruction of gender may explain why feminism has tended to fight for equal opportunities (equality of opportunity despite differences), rather than for the recognition of, and work for, equality and gender deconstruction. 'Equality' may be perceived as equal with men and thus 'like men'. Images of an androgynous population, all looking, dressing, and behaving the same, are not particularly stimulating. However, to me the deconstruction of the gender dichotomy would involve the deconstruction of 'masculine' and 'feminine' qualities and the value system behind this dichotomy. People would be able to behave in ways we have traditionally defined as masculine or feminine but these positions would no longer be gendered, so allowing people more flexibility and experimentation. Many believe already that people all have both masculine and feminine 'sides': deconstructing the gender dichotomy would simply mean that these different ways of being were no longer stigmatised as masculine or feminine. Thus I support Connell's (1987) view that a resulting society would be one of endless diversity rather than sameness. However, this issue is by no means unproblematic, and I return to it in the concluding chapter of this book.

The research

The primary school appeared an appropriate context for my investigation, as studies have catalogued the highly gendered nature of interaction in the primary school classroom and the ways in which children themselves play an active part in constructing their gender identities[8]. I wanted to find out how children went about constructing the genders as different, and the impact these constructions had on their behaviour and power positions in interaction with others. The research was framed around the issue of gender and adult occupation: as the continuing gendered nature of adult work had been one of the issues motivating my research, this seemed an appropriate context within which to investigate children's constructions of gender. Primary school children's stereotyping of adult work has been widely described, as has their gender-stereotypical choice of future occupation[9]. By discussing their constructions of gender and adult work in detail with children, I hoped to discover the types of evidence and discourse children were drawing on in their talk about these issues. Thus while other studies of children's ideas about gender and adult occupation have tended to be based upon interviews and questionnaires which do not address issues of gender discrimination specifically, my research questioned the children directly about gender issues in the classroom and in adult work.

The combination of post-structuralist with feminist, modernist approaches permeates my research aims. For example, I emphasise the social effects of gender discourse, as gender discourse positions men and women in different ways which result in a very real difference in social experiences. I also examine the issue of power: Foucauldian theory of discursive positioning maintains that power resides in discourse and consequently we can all be positioned in discourse as powerful or powerless. However, as the figures discussed earlier show, women still generally perform different tasks in our society and have less access to controlling power than men. From a Foucauldian perspective one cannot quantify whether the generalisation of being a 'girl' or a 'boy' makes a difference to one's interactive power position: the data from my research suggests that it does.

Methods:

A combination of individual interviews and group role-plays were used to observe children's interaction and responses in different discursive environments. I expected to find children providing different responses depending on the research setting, as people draw on different types of discourses depending on who they are communicating with.

Role-Plays

Role-plays were chosen because they appeared an appropriate way to observe and analyse discursive practices and power constructions in child interaction and children's group constructions of gender roles. Groups of four children were asked to conduct role-plays based upon an adult occupational scenario. Building on the group discussion techniques practised by Buckingham (1993) and Bennett (1991), this method provided a means of recording children's interaction and discussion of particular issues within a controlled and easily observable environment.

The choice of role-play contexts were designed based on hospital, hotel or school settings. These contexts were chosen in view of the number of different hierarchical and traditionally gendered occupational positions within them, with which the children might be familiar (through either real life or television). Within each context were four work roles, and a given scenario relating to that occupation, on which to base the play. The scenarios all involved problems to solve, which were intended to provoke discussion among the children in the play. These were:

- *Context*: School

Roles: headteacher, teacher, caretaker, and playground supervisor.

Scenario: the caretaker complains about the amount of litter children were dropping in the playground, and the group hold a meeting to discuss what to do about it.

- *Context*: Hospital.

Roles: doctor, nurse, patient and receptionist.

Scenario: patient complains of receiving inadequate treatment. A group meeting is called to decide what action to take.

- *Context*: Hotel.

Roles: manager, receptionist, chef and room service attendant.

Scenario: a guest has complained to the receptionist that the hotel food was poor and her room was a mess, and a group meeting is called to discuss the problem.

Each group of children selected their occupational context, and then decided among themselves who would play each role. Once this was resolved, they were provided with the work scenario described above. These scenarios were designed to involve everyone and encourage group participation and discussion. Because I was interested in the dynamics and power positionings constructed by the group members during their interaction, I worked with both single-sex and mixed sex groups, to see how constructions of gender and power varied with the gender composition of the group.

An important tenet of feminist research is that research is never 'objective' but reflects or is influenced by the 'standpoint' (social and political position) of the researcher[10]. The researcher's presence in the research is an integral part of it, so should be openly declared. My active participation in the role-plays varied depending on the degree to which children turned to me for direction. If they were quiet and looked to me for assistance I might give them suggestions or ask them questions about their role, to keep the play going and encourage them to participate. Children sometimes appealed to me directly for advice or support and occasionally even included me in their role-play (for instance, giving me a part to play). Thus occasional plays were virtually directed by me, while I hardly participated in others at all: yet my very presence meant that I was involved in the group's interactive constructions.

All but the first four role-plays were video-recorded. It became clear that this was vital for recording the exchanged looks, gesticulations and other forms of non-verbal comment which played an integral part in the group's communication and power construction. The presence of the video-camera on its tall tripod was imposing, and I was concerned at first that it would distract the children. However, although its presence and impact on the interaction and group construction must be acknowledged, it did not appear greatly to influence the nature of the role-plays. For the most part it filled children with interest and excitement when they came into the room, but once they were informed that the film was only for my benefit and given the role-play scenario, they appeared to forget all about it. A small minority of children can be seen smiling coyly at the camera from time to time during the role-play, and a few would demand or beg to watch the film when it was finished, and I would allow them to look at it in replay through the view-finder. However, it was far more common for children to ask to listen to replays of their interviews on my more traditional dictaphone, which suggested that the video-camera had no more effect on the children's interaction than other recording methods.

Interviews

Following the role-play I interviewed each child involved about the role-play interaction and gender issues relating to the school and adult occupation. These were semi-structured interviews, as I was keen to count how many provided certain responses to certain specific questions. However, I also wanted children to feel free to elaborate on their answers or to ask questions of their own, and I also wanted to ask them further questions about the responses they had provided. Semi-structured interviews enabled this, and encouraged an informal, chatty atmosphere.

These individual interviews with the children from the role-play groups provided a different discursive environment and an opportunity to see whether their constructions of gender would change accordingly. The full list of interview questions is shown in Appendix 1. The first group of questions investigated children's own interpretations of the role-play interaction. I then asked each child about their choice of future occupation, whether they thought men and women equally capable at different types of work, and invited them to speculate on issues of gender in the adult work place. The final group of questions related to children's constructions of gender, their talk concerning male and female behaviour, and their experience or observation of sexism in school.

The interviews involved probing children's answers and often asking them to explain the reasoning behind their responses. Although I did not contradict any sexist statements, I did question their justification for such statements and occasionally provided new information which countered their assumptions (for example, that there are male nurses, or female astronauts). I often supported children's anti-sexist statements and was sympathetic to complaints about sexism. So I was much engaged in discussion, rather than running through a set list of questions in a 'detached' manner. The interviewer necessarily plays a joint part in the construction of meaning during the interview. However, studies such as those of Davies (1989, 1993) and Buckingham (1993) also refute assumptions that children's responses can simply be influenced by an adult interviewer in any straightforward way. These researchers found that in some constructions, approval from adults and proven ability to use adult value systems were important for children, while in others they were to be actively scoffed at. In Davies' study (1989) children often vehemently disagreed with her non-sexist statements, and were eager to correct her 'errors' and convert her to a more stereotyped outlook. There were plenty of examples of this during my interviews. The respondent may give a 'required' answer or a deliberately subversive one depending on the discourses they draw upon. Though it is tempting to interpret children's responses as their fixed opinions or attitudes towards gender issues, 'attitudes' and 'opinions' are simply one response produced in a particular interactive environment[11]. Therefore I avoid using the word 'attitude' or 'opinion' to describe children's expressions, and when discussing children's responses I consider them as constructions specific to the interactive environment of the interviews.

While the research was explicitly motivated by feminist aims so did not make claims to objectivity, I sought to produce a useful study. This meant the research analysis could not be purely anecdotal but had to show that the presentation of children's constructions are representative of the whole sample (see Silverman, 1993). Accordingly, counting was used to show how many children responded in particular ways to the core interview questions.

Informal Observation

In all schools where I conducted research I was able to observe the children in the playground at break times. This was not a formal part of my research and it was not rigorous: I observed playground interaction only occasionally and at a distance. Obviously my findings from this are only impressionistic, but this observation was helpful for background information, such as whether girls joined in at football, or who dominated playground space.

The Schools and the Children

The primary schools in this study are all situated in London and have been given pseudonyms. To gain a broad sample of London primary school children they were selected in inner-city, semi-suburban and suburban areas. Two of the schools were situated in inner-city areas; one had a mixed social class intake, as the catchment area includes both owner-occupied housing and many council estates. The fourth school was a Catholic school located in a middle-class suburban area and the others were multi-racial. My data is not analysed according to school, as my aim was to gain a broad cross-section of London primary school children.

One hundred and forty five children took part in the research, and their responses are analysed according to gender and age. Of these, 81 were girls and 64 boys, and the focus was on 7-8 and 10-11 year olds particularly from primary school years Three and Six. I was encouraged to work with different age-groups by Buckingham's (1993) findings that group constructions varied according to age. The 7-8 year olds interested me because it has been argued that children engage in the most vigorous assertion of gender identity between five and seven years of age[12]. Thus I expected the 7-8 year old age group to be just leaving their period of rigorous gender category maintenance. Furthermore, Piaget (1964) argues that it is around the age of seven that ideas of moral and social justice ('fairness') become extremely important to children, and a factor in their constructions. I wanted to see whether these ideas about social justice would affect the children's use of gender discourse. The research also includes four 8-9 year olds, and eight 9-10 year olds. Table 1 shows the number of girls and boys in each age group.

Table 1: Numbers of children in each age group		
	No. of Girls	No. of Boys
AGE 7-8	36	33
AGE 8-9	2	2
AGE 9-10	4	4
AGE 10-11	39	25
TOTAL:	81	64

Although ethnicity was not central to my investigations, I intended my sample to be representative of racial diversity in the various areas of London. Table 2 indicates the number of girls and boys from different ethnic groups

Table 2: Numbers of children from various ethnic groups

	No. of Girls	No. of Boys
South Asian	9	15
African-Caribbean	15	10
Anglo	46	30
Greek-Cypriot	4	3
African	2	1
North African	4	1
South American	0	2
East Asian	1	2
N	81	64

The participants were randomly selected from the returned letters permitting me to interview them. However, my selection was restricted in some instances according to the number of children who returned these letters: for instance, at one school only a small proportion of notes had been returned in the Year Six class, which meant that I could only work with three groups of children from that class. At this school two girls participated in two role-plays, to make up the numbers. Due to the variation in numbers of children given permission to participate in the research from certain classes, eleven children could not be incorporated into role-play groups: the role-plays involved groups of four, so occasionally there were children left over. Rather than exclude these children altogether, interviews were conducted with them.

There were fifteen mixed sex role-play groups, usually two girls and two boys and in one instance three girls and only one boy, as numbers were not even. There were also eleven single-sex girls' groups and eight single-sex boys' groups. (Most of the classes of children I worked with contained more girls than boys, which explains this imbalance.) Table 3 shows the numbers of role-play groups. Differences in number are due

Table 3: Age and gender in the role play groups			
	Mixed Group	Girls' Group	Boys' Group	N
Year Three (7-8 yrs)	6	5	5	16
Year Four (8-9 yrs)	1	0	0	1
Year Five (9-10 yrs)	2	0	0	2
Year Six (10-11 yrs)	6	6	3	15
Total:	15	11	8	34

to the number of girls and boys in each class, permission from parents for the children's participation, and availability. Table 3 also shows the ages of the children involved and the gender make-up of the groups.

Feminist concerns regarding research practice

Feminist writers such as Stanley and Wise (1993) and Maynard and Purvis (1994) have argued that for research to be feminist, the research process itself should be unexploitative. My use of role-play allowed children to choose their own roles and decide the course and lengths of the play, giving them a certain amount of control. Because the interviews were semi-structured, children had space to talk about their own concerns. They often prolonged the interviews in order to chat, ask me questions or confide in me. Their questions were sometimes extremely personal: I was often asked if I had a boyfriend or husband, and about our lives and even whether we slept in the same bed! I made an effort to answer them because they had been prepared to consider and answer my questions: I feel this approach created an atmosphere of mutual respect and put me in a somewhat more equal position to the child than more traditional, 'objective' interview techniques. I also tried to position less as an adult authority figure by using colloquial speech. My responses to the children's answers were subjective (for instance, sympathetically shocked if a child told me about an incident of sexism or bullying) and this seemed to make children more relaxed, because of the supportive atmosphere and chatty informality, and because their contributions were being taken seriously.

Thus my research methods minimised the exploitative atmosphere of a 'scientific experiment'. However, the claim of Stanley and Wise (1993) that researchers should not view or present themselves as intellectually privileged over the researched becomes especially problematic when working with young children: to attempt to maintain such a 'non-privileged' position would obviously involve falsification. Although I tried to portray myself as closer in position to the children than teachers might do, my position as an adult interviewing children remains, and such differences of power and experience inevitably affect the interview. However, children appeared to relish a situation in which their statements are seriously, and confidentially, listened to: this is supported by the findings of Davies (1993) and Skeggs (1994), who argue that children enjoy such respectful conversation and gain a feeling of self-worth when adults take their views seriously. Yet, despite my small concessions to pupil control in the research, power dichotomies between the researcher and the researched cannot be said to have radically altered. As Stanley and Wise (1993) observe:

> ethical issues and dilemmas are solved neither by 'being nice' nor by 'taking research back', because alongside ethical issues and dilemmas concerning the use and abuse of 'subjects' are epistemological issues; these concern whose knowledge, seen in what terms, around whose definitions and standards, and judged by whose as well as what criteria, should count as 'knowledge' itself (p. 202).

Denscombe (1995) notes that the researcher, in ethnographic as much as 'scientific' positivist research, initiates contact with respondents, chooses the setting, selects the interview sample, guides the interview process, takes responsibility for recording events, formally terminates the interviews, and analyses the outcome. My research is no different. Thus I conclude that the best we can do as feminists is to acknowledge these problematic issues in our research and hope that the respondents gain something from it. Certainly the children in my study were extremely keen to participate and appeared greatly to enjoy doing so.

Explicitly discussing gender issues in the interviews raises two ethical concerns. Firstly, for children whose anti-sexist constructions were supported and strengthened through their participation in the research and, secondly, for children whose sexist responses were undermined through their participation. (Of course, participation will have affected children in different ways: some children may have remained unaffected and others might have actually strengthened their sexist constructions by articulating them.) The awareness of children whose anti-sexist statements have been supported has been raised, but as Denscombe (1995) observes, social reality outside the research environment has remained the same, which could leave children vulnerable. An example from my data is a girl's report about two girlfriends whom I had interviewed previously: in their interviews they had complained about the boys' refusal to let them join in at football (and had received my sympathy). According to the first girl, these girlfriends had challenged the boys about this after their interviews, but had again been rejected by the boys. Denscombe suggests that the advantages of greater awareness outweigh such possible disappointments. The issues of children whose sexist constructions may have been undermined are more problematic: as Denscombe points out, while 'giving voice' to those who share the researcher's constructions, the voice of those whose responses differ can be repressed. Thus Denscombe concludes that 'emancipatory research' cannot necessarily be said to benefit all participants, and may still be experienced as oppressive by some. While such considerations would not deter me from my feminist intentions, such points ought at least to be acknowledged.

'Race' and social class

Ethnicity has been shown to have an impact on research: it affects the discourses one has recourse to, and positions of power within discourse[13]. White feminists have been criticised for ignoring this issue (or viewing racial discrimination as interchangeable with gender discrimination) in the past[14]. While my research did not focus on the black community but on children from different ethnic groups in a primary school context, power positionings concerning race inevitably impacted on my interviews with children from ethnic minority groups. So besides gender, class and age, race was another factor affecting the power dynamics between me and my respondents in my interviews with children, and that this must have affected discourses drawn on by my respondents. I was concerned that my research should acknowledge the existence of all ethnic groups, rather than ignoring the existence of 'non-whites' in my research, or marginalising ethnic minorities and presenting them as Other (Phoenix, 1987). Likewise, social class has also been found to impact on children's discourses (Walkerdine, 1997; Walkerdine and Lucey, 1989). Analysis of children's use of discourse according to race and social class (besides gender) was beyond the scope of this study but it would constitute important further research concerning children's discursive power constructions.

Transcript Convention

The transcripts conventions used in my reproduction of the interview and role-play data are shown in Figure 1.

Figure 1

(.)   Short pause.

(2)   Pause of two seconds duration (number changes to indicate length of pause in seconds).

=   To indicate lack of pause between speakers; for instance when one speaker gives way to another.

[
[To indicate two or more people speaking at the same time.

Italics To indicate emphasised words

....   Inaudible speech.

{}   Descriptive addition, e.g. {giggling}

:   To indicate a long, drawn out word, e.g. No:o

[ ]   My addition, for instance explaining what someone is referring to.

( )   Descriptive addition to observe gestures, expressions, and the direction and object of speech (i.e. to record who a person is talking to).

All the children's names have been changed and replaced with gender and ethnicity-appropriate alternatives. Whenever I refer to individual children or their transcripts, a coded identification follows their names, representing their gender and age. Thus 'Claudette (F, 10)' describes Claudette who is female (F), and ten years of age (10).

The rest of the book

The rest of the book concentrates on the children's constructions of gender. Chapter Two illustrates the ways in which children construct the genders as different in their talk, and I argue that many children went further still, actually constructing the genders as oppositional in the classroom. In Chapter Three I discuss the children's talk about adult occupation, looking at how they draw upon, or reject, traditional gender stereotypes, and the reasoning behind their arguments.

The following chapters examine the effect that children's constructions of gender had on their behaviour and power positions. Chapter Four returns to children's constructions of gender in their own lives, showing how their descriptions of sexist incidents in the classroom were linked to their constructions of the genders as oppositional. Chapter Five describes how the oppositional constructions of gender encouraged children to behave in particular ways, creating symbolic masculine and feminine cultures in the classroom. In Chapter Six I argue that these oppositional positions led to a gendered imbalance of power during the children's role-play interaction; as the girls' constructed feminine positions led to the abdication of power to the boys.

The conclusion that children's gender constructions had a very real impact on their power positions during interaction led me to investigate the types of gender discourse and other evidence that children were drawing on in their talk about gender issues. In Chapter Seven the different gender narratives evident in children's speech are teased out and analysed, and the different sources of evidence on gender issues (e.g. family, television) are investigated. The ways children used evidence to support gender discourses are identified, showing how stereotypical and counter-stereotypical evidence can be either utilised or rejected. And finally in Chapter Eight I summarise my findings, linking them with some contemporary issues about girls' and boys' respective success in the education system. I conclude that to address and disrupt the gendered power differences amongst children we must strive to deconstruct the gender dichotomy. This will be extremely difficult and presents a challenge to us all: educators, as well as students, have desire and power invested in the traditional gender constructions. But there are some ways that teachers can contribute to children's questioning of the gender dichotomy and these are suggested. Perhaps by engaging with these issues with children we may help not only to provide new discursive possibilities for them but also to learn more about our own gender constructions.

Notes

1. See the Equal Opportunities Commission Report (1996), their *Briefings on Women and Men in Britain* (1997), and *The Times Educational Supplement* (29/11/95), for elaboration on female educational and academic achievements.

2. Foucault's *Madness and Civilisation* (1967) is a particularly strong example of this exclusive type of writing. For more readable examples of his work, see *Power/Knowledge* (1980), or the various volumes of *History of Sexuality* (1972).

3. See, for example, Griffiths (1995); Ramazanoglu (1993); Fraser and Nicholson (1990).

4. The 'enlightenment' refers to the Renaissance period, where post-structuralist and feminist writers believe modernist beliefs concerning human project, human progression, and scientific, 'rational' truth originated.

5. Sandra Harding (1984;1991) has written widely and lucidly on this issue.

6. The work of Shotter (1993) and Billig (1987, 1992; Billig *et al,* 1988) describes how we think and speak in multiple and contradictory ways. Billig, particularly, argues that talk is dilemmatic and rhetorical and that as we articulate one argument, we simultaneously evoke knowledge of a counter-argument.

7. Notable exceptions include Davies (1989, 1993), Connell (1987, 1995) and Jones (1993).

8. See the studies by Thorne (1993); Steedman (1982); Lloyd and Duveen (1992); and Adams and Walkerdine (1986) on gender in the primary school.

9. Nemerowicz (1979), Adams and Walkerdine (1986), Rosenthal and Chapman (1982) and Tremaine (1982) show how children stereotype occupations according to gender and the studies of Robb (1981), Adams and Walkerdine (1986) and Spender (1982) illustrate the how children's own career choices are gendered.

10. See the work of Stanley and Wise (1993) and Maynard (1994) for an explanation of this argument.

11. Potter and Wetherell (1987) and Lave and Wenger (1991) have discussed how apparently fixed attitudes and opinion cannot be divorced from the particular social environment in which they are produced.

12. See Lloyd and Duveen (1992); Damon (1977); Kohlberg (1966); Davies (1989)

13. The authors of *The Empire Strikes Back* (Centre for Contemporary Cultural Studies, 1982) claim that white researchers cannot gain or interpret meaningful responses from black respondents, and Marshall (1994) and Phoenix (1987, 1994) describe how ethnicity impacts upon the construction between interviewer and respondents from different ethnic groups.

14. See hooks (1982, 1989); Phoenix (1987), for elaboration.

CHAPTER 2

CHILDREN'S TALK ABOUT GENDER IN THEIR SCHOOL LIVES

This chapter investigates children's responses when interviewed about gender in their lives at school. Gender category maintenance, we have seen, has been found important for perpetuating the gender dichotomy and maintaining stable gender identities. In their observational studies of primary classrooms, Davies (1989) and Jordan (1995) catalogue the ways in which gender is actively constructed, accommodated, resisted and manipulated by children, and argue that gender is constructed by children as *relational*. As masculinity is defined by its difference to femininity, so the genders are constructed as two relational groups. Data presented in this chapter supports this, although there were occasions when children constructed the genders as different but not necessarily *relational* to one another. For example, children might construct it as acceptable for girls to play with all kinds of dolls, but not for boys to play with any dolls apart from Action Men: this constructs the genders as different but not as relational. The first part of this chapter deals with these presentations of the genders as different, illustrating how children achieved this in their talk.

Certain constructions went further still. Thorne (1993) observes that children sometimes construct 'the girls' and 'the boys' as rival groups. I found that children often used gender category maintenance to construct the genders as *oppositional*: either in opposition (as in a 'battle of the sexes'), or as polar opposites, an idea that is developed later.

I asked the children questions relating to their constructions of gender:

'Do girls and boys behave differently in class or not?' and

'Are girls and boys just acting differently, or are they really different inside?'

The first question aimed to discover whether or not children presented classroom interaction as gendered, and (if they said that the genders *do* behave differently) what the differences were. The second question sought to find out whether they presented differences as due to superficial or to inherent disparities between the sexes, in a sense asking them their views on the 'nature or nurture' debate on gender!

Yes! the genders behave differently

In response to the question 'Do girls and boys behave differently in class or not?', 95% of the girls and 75% of the boys provided affirmative answers. When asked whether the genders are simply acting differently or are really different inside, around a third of children said they did not know or did not respond. However, over a third of children said that girls and boys are really different inside (see Table 1).

These figures suggest a general consensus that the genders behave in different ways in school. However, there is an age difference in the children's constructions: far more children in the older group suggested that gender differences are superficial than did their younger counter-

Table 1: Are girls and boys just acting differently, or are they really different inside?				
	AGE 7-8		10-11	
	girls	boys	girls	boys
	%	%	%	%
different inside	47	36	25	28
just acting differently	25	24	49	40
don't know and no response	28	40	26	32
N	36	33	39	25

parts – most of whom said that boys and girls are different inside. The younger children's greater support of the idea that the genders are inherently different could be seen as part of gender category maintenance. Psychologists such as Damon (1977), Durkin (1985) and Lloyd and Duveen (1992) argue that rigid adherence to gender roles so as to maintain gender identity is most rigorous between the ages of five and seven. Young children do not yet comprehend the permanency of biologically assigned sex, and so visual display of a relational gender dichotomy is particularly important to them at this age to secure their gender identity. But by the age of seven children usually understand that sex is fixed, and at this point they begin to refine and elaborate their understanding of gender issues (Durkin, 1985). Gender category maintenance therefore decreases at this age and continues to do so until adolescence. The older children may be less keen to assign types of behaviour as inherently gendered. However, the evidence for such changes in children's gender constructions is limited and inconclusive. For instance, having conducted research with pre-school children, Davies and Banks (1992) and Davies (1993) interviewed some of them again in their later primary school years and found their constructions scarcely changed.

When discussing the questions about gender and behaviour and other matters, children often talked as though there is a clear dichotomy between the sexes. This supports Davies' (1989) suggestion that children take up gender positions as though the two genders are relational. I found that they constructed the genders as visually and behaviourally different and often inter-related these differences in their constructions.

Use of visual signs and behaviour to construct the genders as different

In the children's talk visual *signs* of gender, involving stereotypically gendered accessories, clothes and behaviour, play a crucial part in children's construction of gender identity. Children take these up as signifiers of their gender allegiance.

Clothes are important indicators of gender identity. When I ask Zoe (F, 7) whether boys behave differently to girls in her class, she replies, "Yeah, because boys don't wear skirts, or kni-knickers, or mini-skirts or belly-tops or, or that sort of stuff (.) and they don't wear ribbons in their hair". The link between clothes and gendered behaviour is emphasised when I ask Zoe *why* boys do not wear those clothes, and she replies (laughing at my question), 'Because (2) *they* like, like *Streetfighter 2* and like *wrestlers*, and say, *Oh, Yeah*'. Such visual behaviour (watching macho films and sports, and using particular phrases) is still connected to outward appearance and signs, and Zoe poses boys' engagement with these as the reason boys do not wear 'feminine' clothes. Gender-typed clothing was taken up almost as a part of one's gender. For example, Somina (F, 11) maintains that women cannot be builders because they wear dresses, and when I point out that women can wear trousers Somina replies, 'Ye- yeah, but, like, they don't um (.) they don't feel very good with trousers on, or something, like *they* [men] do'. Thus women cannot perform the traditionally masculine job of builder because they wear dresses, and dresses appear here as part of the identity of being a woman. Similarly, Zoe (F, 7) claims that to be a builder a woman would have to 'dress up as a boy'. The gender dichotomy appears so fixed in Zoe's construction that to take up a traditionally male role a woman must actually appear to be a male.

These findings echo Davies' (1989) argument that gender is a public achievement. Similarly, Thorne (1993) points out that where gender boundaries are evoked by children, they are often accompanied by ritualised or stylised forms of action: a visual show. Catia (F, 8), a keen cyclist, points out the connection with clothing and identity when complaining about having to wear a dress as part of her school uniform: 'in this dress you wouldn't think I like cycling, would you?' It seems that her dress identifies her with non-physical pursuits. Catia observes that children look different when wearing their school uniform. Similarly Rebecca (F, 8) tells how she convinced some boys that she could play football by scoring a goal in high-heeled shoes: these shoes appear linked to the boys' accusation that she was too 'girly-girly' to play, and Rebecca's pride is based upon the fact that she scored a goal *despite* wearing them. Both these examples also demonstrate the link between feminine clothes and an inability to engage in physical pursuits: as well as signalling a gender difference, the clothes actively enforce it by encumbering girls and reducing their ability to engage in 'masculine' activity. By encouraging girls to wear dresses or skirts as part of school uniform, schools help to enforce this situation. Regarding the link between outward signs and gender identity, the following extract from Zoe's (F, 7) transcript is revealing. Having pointed out that girls wear different clothes from boys, she continues:

Z: But there's *one* girl in our class who wants to be a boy, and there's my friend called Rosanne, and she dresses as a boy, she won't have *anything* in her hair

I: Does she? what do you think about that?

Z: Erm (2) *strange*

I: Strange (.) but you don't mind, or do you?

Z: Mm, don't really *mind*, but (.) *Sarah* says that she's a boy, but *I* don't really believe her

So what you wear can indicate your identity – Sarah claims that she *is* a boy, not just that she would prefer to be one. While Zoe says that she does not believe Sarah, she offers an uncertain and hesitant quali-fication, 'really' ('I don't really believe her'), suggesting that she has at least considered the legitimacy of Sarah's claim. This illustrates both how outward signs of gender depict gender identity, and why gender category maintenance is so important for children: Sarah's claim that she is a boy, despite her biological sex, shows how easily gender can be thrown into doubt, so presenting a challenge to the gender dichotomy and thus to the gender identities of other children.

The conversation continued:

I: Do you think there's a good reason to want to be a boy, for a girl? {Zoe shakes her head} (.) no, how come?

Z: Because (.) I think girls are good enough

I: Yes

Z: They might like, girls are much more, like, if you're, if you don't beat up people you're more like girls, and, like if you *hurt*, if you hurt each other that's *not* more like, girls, and, like this girl called Sarah in my class –

I: Mm

Z: She says that, she's gonna do play fighting today, and I don't think *that's* very good *either*

Zoe's rejection of the validity of girls trying to be boys raises a complex issue. Rather than rejecting the aspiration to maleness because it is 'wrong' or 'unnatural', Zoe argues that 'girls are good enough', implying that her girlfriends want to be boys because they see males as superior, and that she is defending girlhood against this sexist suggestion. From this perspective, Sarah and Rosanne are presented as traitors to girlhood, and Zoe's visual femininity as solidarity with girlhood. She supports her claim that 'girls are good enough' with the example of the negativity of male violence, suggesting that girls do not 'beat up people' and criticising Sarah for her engagement in 'play fighting'. However, this criticism of Sarah's behaviour could also be interpreted as gender category maintenance on Zoe's part.

Often gender-appropriate behaviour, or gender itself, appeared very much connected with visual signs in children's constructions. For example, Yve (F, 8) explains that boys behave differently from girls because boys 'spit on the ground'. The difference in children's toys according to gender was often referred to (boys so often alluding to Barbie dolls that one could suggest a male yearning for this media-hyped toy). Lloyd and Duveen (1992) have demonstrated that children categorise toys by gender, and Dixon (1990) and Delamont (1980) have argued that gender-typed toys socialise children into traditional gender roles. I support Lloyd and Duveen's (1992) finding that children actively take up these gender-typed toys as signs of their gender identity, much as children take up particular playground games to affirm gender distinction, as observed by Thorne (1993). Rather than being persuaded to take up such forms of play by the forces of socialisation, children use such toys actively to demonstrate their gender.

Masculinity has also to be achieved[1]. In his observation of primary school boys' discussion groups, Buckingham (1993) shows how they can mutually support one another's fragile constructs of masculinity. There are several instances in my data concerning such gender maintenance which demonstrate the immense pressure that conformity to masculine culture places on boys. Listening to their parents gave me insights into aspects of some children's lives which the children themselves might not have revealed to me. Shofic's (M, 7) mother told me that Shofic hates defeat, particularly by girls, and said that he had been too embarrassed to tell her about a serious incident when four girls overpowered him and tied him up in the playground (the incident had been relayed to her by teachers). Tim's (M, 11) mother told me that he had saved up for weight-training equipment himself and devised his own rigorous training programme because he is so self-conscious about his small size. Apparently, lack of physical strength or being over-powered by supposedly 'weaker' girls can undermine the fragile masculine identity. Jordan (1995) argues that boys construct masculinity by positioning themselves as 'Other' to 'wimpy' boys as well as girls: thus failure to achieve 'proper masculinity' bears the risk of being relegated to the status of 'girl'. This extract from my interview with Leke (M, 7), is illustrative:

I: Do you think in your class, um girls act differently to boys?

L: Uh, girls play with dolls and boys play with, toys, but I would like to be a girl

I: Would you?

L: Yeah, because girls have more toys and Barbies, what do boys have? those crush dummy things, stupid things {laughs}

I: Yes, why can't you play with Barbies when you're a boy?

L: (.) Cos the girls do

I: Mm, do you play with Barbies at all or not?

L: (.) Nah

I: No (.) just cos they're girl's things?

L: Well, you can get Barbie *men*

I: Yes (.) what do you think, I mean what   [wouldpeople think=

L: [Like, with the Barbie Men

      Car innit, you have to have the *pink* one

I: Yeah (.) what do you think people would think if you *did* play with Barbies?

L: (.) They'd think I'm a gay

I: Yeah, why – why would that be though?

L: Cos girls' things are for girls and boys' things are for boys

I: Wh- do you think that's fair though? (.) what about girls playing football and things like that, should they be able to play football?

L: Yeah

I: Yeh

L: A lot of girls don't like playing basketball, because they think that basketball's only for girls

I: For boys, you mean

L: For boys, I mean

I: But it's not, is it?

L: No

I: But the thing is, some girls *do* play football and basketball don't they, so wouldn't it be fair if boys were allowed to play with dolls and things as well?

L: *Yeah*

I: Mm (.) do you think that one day it'll be like that?

L: Yeah

Leke's interest in, and wish to play with, dolls is quite clear; to the extent that he declares he would like to be a girl. However, he is adamant that being a boy and playing with dolls is not possible: the crossing of gender boundaries is prevented by a strong form of gender category maintenance involving the censuring fear of being called 'gay' – in other words, being defined as *not properly masculine*. Thus Leke, who presents himself in a very 'hard' masculine manner, is forced to repress his yearnings for feminine expression.

Many of the examples above demonstrate the inter-related nature of gendered visual signs and gendered behaviour: for example, a girl playing with a doll is taking up a visual sign of her gender identity and engaging in gendered behaviour. According to many of the children, boys behave in different ways to girls and are interested in different things. They presented the genders as behaving distinctly in the classroom. Many observational studies in the primary classroom have reported differences in behaviour between girls and boys, generally describing boys as rowdy, disruptive, and preoccupied with violence. Conversely, girls are observed in similar research to be diligent, sensible and quiet[2]. When I asked children whether they thought girls behaved differently to boys in school (and vice versa) the children often supported these descriptions. Indeed, they universally generalised about 'the boys' and 'the girls', almost as though they were two separate species. I was of course evoking the gender dichotomy by asking whether the behaviour of the two sexes was different in the classroom, and this may have produced a particularly generalising response. However, the differences in behaviour the children most often mentioned were those previously observed by feminist researchers. Reports included: boys 'muck about more' than girls (Mark, M, 11), boys in the class are naughtier than girls (Cathleen, F, 7), 'boys shout a lot, and girls don't' (Lesley, F, 7), and boys 'muck around' and fight more (Paulina, F, 10). Concerning the girls, children reported that: 'the girls behave more properly than the boys' (Lucinda, F, 7), girls are 'more sensible' (Marguerite, F, 7), and girls work harder and talk less than boys (Robert, M, 7). The children appeared to be constructing the classroom behaviour of boys and girls as fundamentally different.

The 'sensible-selfless/silly-selfish' gender dichotomy

There is a further issue. In her observational study of primary school girls, Belotti (1975) observes that girls worked diligently, neatly and conscientiously, in an attempt to impress and win the approval of the teacher. Belotti argues that girls aimed to be viewed as mature, well-behaved and sensible. The boys in her study apparently did not share these concerns. They were naughty, immature and messy. This resulted in the boys gaining most of the teacher's attention, and girls often clearing up after the boys in their efforts to gain the teacher's appreciation. Walkerdine (1990) analyses this phenomenon more fully and she argues that child-centred discourses in education have created an image of the school as a 'facilitating environment' catering for the needs of 'the child' (usually assumed to be a male). The child is the individual, whose needs must be met by the teacher (usually female): the teacher simply becomes part of the child's facilitating environment. Thus a dichotomy forms:

teacher – child
passive – active
feminine – masculine

According to Walkerdine there is no position for girls to take up as active child: they can take up the position of 'feminine object of masculine gaze', or of quasi-teacher – which involves identification with the teacher in the way that Belotti catalogues. Girls become 'mature' and self-consciously hard-working, trying to behave like the teacher or as the teacher seems to expect, so as to win her approval. Girls who do not conform to this behaviour are often penalised more heavily by teachers than are boys: boys' naughtiness is perceived as 'natural', whereas naughty girls are 'little madams'[3]. Ironically however, studies have shown that girls rarely win the teacher's favour through their selfless behaviour and that some teachers indeed actively disdain such behaviour[4].

Thus Walkerdine and Belotti present children taking up polarised gender positions. Drawing on their findings as well as my own (see Francis, 1998a) I have named these dichotomous constructions the 'sensible selfless' (feminine) and 'silly selfish' (masculine) positions. Of the feminine construction, maturity, obedience and neatness are the valued 'sensible' qualities, which naturally lead to 'selflessness' – giving and facilitating. The masculine construction involves 'silly' qualities of immaturity, messiness and naughtiness, leading to 'selfishness' – taking and demanding. Notions of what sensible or silly behaviour constitutes within the classroom environment are obviously culturally grounded and produced in a particular educational/adult-child discourse. However, anyone who has worked in primary school will be familiar with these constructions and with the forms of behaviour associated with them (Clarricoates, 1980, has shown how many teachers even expect such gendered modes of behaviour from children). 'Sensible' and 'silly' were the words used frequently by the children themselves when describing gendered behaviour. Connell (1995) argues that there are different forms of masculinity and femininity but that certain forms have become 'hegemonic' (dominant and perpetuated as dominant) in society. The hegemonic forms often draw on the gender dichotomy (for instance, males as rational and strong, women as emotive and weak). People do not necessarily achieve or maintain the hegemonic form of gender all the time. I suggest that the sensible-selfless (female) and silly-selfish (male) constructions represented the hegemonic forms of masculinity and femininity amongst primary school children. It is this dichotomous construction of the genders which is being reflected in the children's talk about classroom behaviour. These constructions and their impact on children's interaction are discussed more fully in the fifth chapter.

Children's construction of genders as oppositional

Drawing on this dichotomous construction, many children went even further and actually constructed the genders as *oppositional*, by presenting them either as in opposition or as opposite. The construction of the two genders as opposite to one another was common. So while the children referred to above maintained that, for instance, the boys are rougher than the girls or that the girls work harder than the boys, some other children suggest that the two groups actually behave in opposite ways. For example, Salim (M, 10) says that, 'boys behave a bit rough and girls behave a bit sensible', and Catia (F, 8) observes that males are competitive (like to 'rush ahead'), whereas females prefer to do things collectively. Lucinda (F, 7) presents the two gender groups as opposite, declaring, 'girls are good and the boys are bad'. Other children depicted the genders as in opposition, evoking a 'battle of the sexes'. For example, Rebecca (F, 8) observes that, 'the women think that *girls* are the best, and the men think that the boys are the best, like every time a baby's born they say I wish it's a boy (.) or I wish it's a girl', and Veronica (F, 7) claims that boys hate girls and that she hates boys.

So my findings offer support for Davies' (1989) argument – that in a society where everyone is positioned as male or female and where one's gender is an integral part of one's social self, the taking up of gender signifiers and the maintenance of these is very important for children. My findings also suggest that oppositional constructions may result from children's construction of gender as relational as they take up dichotomous forms of behaviour to signify their gender identity.

However, the ways in which children constructed gender was in no way unitary, as Zoe's report of Sarah's behaviour demonstrates.

Girls and boys are 'just acting differently'

Despite the large number of children who opted for the response that girls and boys are different inside, a similar proportion (37% of girls and 31% of boys; see Table 1), stated that the genders are not different inside. Many of these children said differences in behaviour between boys and girls at primary school are 'put on' for various reasons. Some argued that gendered differences in behaviour are due to constructions about acceptable modes of behaviour for girls and boys: Vanessa explains of boys, 'Like if someone died they can't – when they wanna cry they keep it in cos they say Oh only women cry and babies'. It was usually *boys'* behaviour that was used as an example of this by both girls and boys, suggesting that it is their modes of masculinity which are most noticed by children to be socially constructed. For example, Salim (M, 11) observes that boys often like and admire girls but when boys talk to girls, despite their best intentions, 'they start messing about, they don't like her, they start swearing at them and stuff' because they are embarrassed in front of their friends. Paulina (F, 10) argues that boys think girls are attracted by a show of masculinity, so try to act accordingly:

I: Why do you think boys do things like that, like tease girls?

P: Well, y'know just to show that they're big and tough

I: But they're not all bigger are they?

P: No

I: And why's it so good to be tough, for them?

P: I, I dunno really, y'know, makes everyone think Oh wow, he's so tough, an', y'know, really I think, that the only reason why boys act that way, yeah? is cos they think girls like it (.) they think the girls will like them being big and strong, and –

I: Mm, and do you think the girls do like it?

P: Well, some do, but not all (.) I mean really, a girl would only like a boy, y'know like really, like my mum, she's known this guy for a long long time since she was a little girl, and she really likes him

I: Yep

P: So you know, if you've known someone for a very long time and you really love them and that, that's love (.) not if, y'know, someone beats someone up and then Ahhh, y'know, He's so *spectacular*

This 'macho' behaviour was pointed to by many children to demonstrate the way boys deliberately act in a certain way in order to impress, although the majority of these children identified the motive to be impressing male friends, rather than girls as Paulina suggests. Samantha (F, 11) argues this point in the following extract, claiming that the boys' competitiveness and silliness simply shows their efforts to impress their male friends:

S: I think they [boys] just want attention

I: Mm (.) why do they want attention when girls don't, though?

S: I don't know, quite a lot of boys are show-offs and want to be the best

I: (.) M, yeh

S: And show their friends that they can do everything

I: Why do you think girls don't need that so much though?

S: Cos if you've got proper friends you don't really have to do that

I: And boys don't?

S: Well, I think boys think that they have to like, pass a test to be with their friends, or something like that

Vanessa (F, 11) explains of boys, 'they try not to cry because they're scared of what their friends might say, Oh you're a baby, and things'. Thus she both identifies boys' repression of their emotions as socially motivated and demonstrates an awareness of the social pressures and policing which children engage in concerning gender roles. This report of Vanessa's alludes to an instance of gender category maintenance and a number of other children gave similar examples. Gender category maintenance, then, is recognised as a social construction by many children and such gendered social constructions are presented as every-day aspects of school/childhood life. So many children, particularly in the older age group (see Table 1), presented gender differences as superficial or 'put on'.

Children's construction of girls and boys as the same

Few boys, and even fewer girls, said that boys and girls do not behave differently in the classroom. Of those who did say that there is no gender difference in behaviour (see Table 1), many went on to present the genders as different later in their interviews. However, seven boys (11%) and four girls (5%) consistently constructed the genders as the same throughout their interviews, maintaining that there is no difference between girls and boys in terms of behaviour or ability. A number of children questioned and resisted the gender dichotomy in their interviews, often pointing to its over-generalisation, observing that boys do not *all* behave one way, and girls another. Lynn (F, 7) suggests that girls ostracise boys because, 'they probably think that all boys are the same as Andrew, cos he's really silly 'n' they probably think that they're all like that'. She says that this generalisation is inaccurate. When asked whether girls are different from boys, Charity (F, 11) replies, '*some* of them are the same, *some* of them are, completely different'. She goes on to explain that some girls and boys are keen to try the same activities. Catia (F, 8) observes that girls are different from one another, saying 'some girls, they like to be like *girls,* but some girls, they want to be on their bikes' (the latter type includes Catia). I asked if these differences matter and Catia replied that she does not think it matters, but, 'It's just that the girls who don't want to be on their bikes and want to be *girls*, they say {whingey voice} Act like a girl, not like a boy (.) it's not fair on me because, my friends, they're like, *girls'* girls, and they hardly ever go out on their bikes'.

Catia is not like Sarah and Rosanne (discussed above) who apparently want to be like boys – she simply appears to find the gender category maintenance of the '*girls*' girls' trying and restricting. Catia also explains how boys claim to be stronger than girls but points out that she has seen a girl who is stronger than boys, concluding that the generalisation is unfounded. Seven girls (9%) and two boys (3%) objected to over-generalisation concerning behavioural and physical differences between genders, and the expectation that people will conform to these stereotypes. While only a small number of children argued that there are no differences in behaviour between genders or directly questioned the gender dichotomy, they were a vocal minority. These children show that even when answering interview questions which evoked the gender dichotomy, a discursive possibility is open to some children which allows them to deny or challenge that dichotomy. The majority of children who did so were from the older age group: only four were from Year Three. Again, this may be due to higher gender category maintenance amongst the younger children.

Contradictions within children's constructions of a gender dichotomy

Children's constructions of gender were not unitary but fluctuated and revealed contradictions. For instance, Michael (M, 7) describes how his friendship with Samantha overrides gender boundaries:

M: Well, well sometimes, like my *friend*, right, Samantha, right, she, um she plays boy games, and if I want her to, boy games – if she's playing boy games (.) then other times, I play *girl* games

I: Right, so you can be with her=

M: *Yeah*

I: Your mate, yup, yup

M: So when I swap over, she swaps over as well, so then I swap over again

Michael appears to have no qualms about engaging in 'girls' games', thus resisting gender boundaries. Yet he still refers to a clearly defined dichotomy of 'girls' games' and 'boys' games' – the assumptions of gender difference still remain unchallenged in his discourse. Contradiction and resistance does not necessarily mean that the construction of difference is contested. Indeed, it was sometimes surprising to see how far the hegemonic construction of gender duality could contain contradiction without the construction being challenged. A further example is my interview with Leon (M, 7), who generalises about inferior female strength throughout our discussion of gender and adult work, yet later surprised me by his description of playground games. He claims that the girls are selfish because they do not let the boys join in at their games and I ask him which games these are:

I: What do the girls play that's different from the boys?

L: They play, they play um um um *rough* games, that, um, y'know, some games of tennis where you bash the ball {makes bashing noise}, could get in someone's eye –

I: Is this the boys now? or the girls?

L: Thass the girls

I: The girls, yeah (.) so they play rougher games than the boys? don't they let
     the boys play?

L: Yeh

I: Right (.) and what do the boys play?

L: They play kind of er, they play big games, sometimes they play football (.)
     it's hard, sometimes it's very hard tackling, but, but they're so tough they
     can take it, but Tenac's not tough, every time 'e gets knocked over, {I laugh}
     one little knock over, and 'e's crying

I: {laughs} So which is tougher then, playing football, or playing the girl's
     games like tennis and that?

L: (.) Tennis is tougher

Leon's assertion that women are weaker than men and thus not strong
enough to perform manual work had led me to assume that he constructed girls as weaker and less robust than boys. My confusion shows
when I ask whether it is the boys or the girls he is describing: I found
it hard to equate the idea of male physical superiority with his construction of the girls' tennis games as rough ('tougher' than the boys'
games). However, he persists in stating that tennis is 'tougher'. This
contradiction did not appear problematic to Leon. Evidently the
dominant construction of genders as different has the capacity to
contain such contradiction without serious disruption or challenge.

Discussion

Children tend to take up our societal construction of gender as different
in their talk about gender in their own lives and often apply this construction to their classmates. Visual signs and behaviour which signify
gender identity are used by children in a painstaking endeavour to
achieve a gender position. Some children talked about a separation into
competing genders, presenting the genders as in opposition (for
instance, Denzel (M, 7) states, 'Girls *and* boys think they're better than
each other'). The genders were also presented as opposite to one
another, many children articulating a dichotomy where boys are silly

and naughty and girls are sensible and hard-working. These behavioural differences manifest in the formation of two separate, albeit fluid and shifting, gender cultures. Thorne (1993) argues against use of the term 'gender cultures' claiming that social psychologists have used this concept to suggest fixed, essential gender groups, but it seems an apt description of the manifestation of children's polarised gender constructions.

It is important to note two other possible reasons for the construction of gender cultures amongst school children, besides children's own constructions of the genders as oppositional. The first is the way that some aspects of school life mark gender. For instance, the allocation of separate facilities for girls and boys: Tanvier (M, 7) observes that girls and boys are not allowed to share the same changing rooms. Teachers often refer to children as 'the girls' or 'the boys', and categorise them accordingly[5]. So the construction of symbolic gender cultures may be encouraged by the school environment. A second explanation often noted by children for the segregation between genders so evident in schools, is the taboo of sexual/romantic relations between opposite sexes. A girl or boy playing or forming a friendship with a child of different gender is often accused of 'fancying' them and becomes open to ridicule. Salim (M, 10) reports this to be a strong factor in children's reluctance or hesitancy to mix with the opposite sex. This is supported by Thorne's study (1993) which found children giving similar explanations for their gender-segregation.

Although many children constructed gender as different and even oppositional, the gender dichotomy was by no means straightforwardly accepted and taken up in children's interview discussions. Constructions were not unitary but shifted in talk and sometimes contained resistance and contradiction. Some children consistently argued that children do not behave differently according to gender. But the construction of genders as different and relational is the most common among the children I interviewed (mirroring society at large). And the capacity of this dominant construction to contain contradiction without itself being disrupted or challenged appears to be a cause for feminist concern. Clearly, token arguments and examples of similarity between genders will not be sufficient to challenge this powerful, dominant construction of the genders as different. It is by building on this construction of the genders as different that many children go on to construct the genders as oppositional.

Notes

1) See, for example, Buckingham (1993); Middleton (1992); Edley and Wetherell (1995).

2) Spender (1980; 1982) and Haworth et al (1992) describe boys as rowdy; Sarah (1980), Spender (1982) and Riddell (1989) describe them as disruptive, and Vicks (1990) and Haworth et al (1992) observe them to be preoccupied with violence. Conversely, girls are observed in similar research to be diligent (Spender, 1982; Belotti, 1975; Walkerdine, 1988), school-oriented (Lightbody et al, 1996), sensible and quiet (Walkerdine, 1990; Belotti, 1975).

3) Clarricoates (1980), and Spender (1982) found girls are penalised for transgression more heavily than boys in school; presumably because their behaviour is seen to be shockingly unfeminine, or is less expected on the part of the teacher.

4) See Stanworth (1981), Spender (1982), Sharpe (1976), Clarricoates (1980), and Walkerdine (1990) for accounts of this.

5) Lloyd and Duveen (1992), Holland (1981), Whyte (1986), Thorne (1993), and Sealey and Knight (1990), are some of the many feminist researchers that have described the ways in which teachers use genders to categorise and form their perceptions about children.

CHAPTER 3

CHILDREN'S TALK ABOUT GENDER AND ADULT WORK

This chapter examines children's constructions of gender and adult occupation and whether they envisaged gender discrimination in the adult workplace. Children were questioned about their choices of future occupation and about hypothetical scenarios concerning gender and adult work.

Children's sex-typing and choice of future adult occupations has been the focus of previous research. Nemerowicz (1979), Robb (1981), Rosenthal and Chapman (1982), Tremaine (1982) and Adams and Walkerdine (1986) have investigated primary school children's allocation of different jobs to different genders and found a high degree of sex-stereotyping on the part of both sexes. These studies all involved children filling in questionnaires in which they were asked to assign different occupations to men or women or to both sexes. I suggest that their findings could have been influenced by the questionnaire format: it normally presented a list of different jobs and boxes where you assigned each one as a job performed by men, by women or by both. Children might see such allocation choices as a kind of test – allocation as 'men's job' is the first option, with 'women's job' second and 'can be done by men and women' presented last. Thus children may see the latter as a last resort answer if the job cannot be properly gendered, rather than seeing it as a primary response. This may at least partially account for their highly gender-stereotypical responses.

Short and Carrington (1989) used qualitative interview techniques instead of questionnaires when asking primary school children about men or women's ability to perform different jobs. Although their findings still revealed a high level of gender stereotyping, the children's answers were less stereotyped than those given in studies using questionnaires. Short and Carrington showed children a sequence of pictures depicting a woman fixing a car and asked them to comment on them. If children did not allude to the 'role reversal', Short and Carrington asked them whether there was anything unusual about the pictures (which, I argue, may have been suggestive and consequently elicited a particularly gender stereotypical response). Their study found that gendered occupational differences were seen as highly significant by children: primary school boys listed better job choice as the second best thing about being male (following greater physical strength).

The questions I asked children about adult work were:

1) What job would you like to do when you leave school?

2) Do men and women have the ability to do all jobs?

3) Are men or women *better* at certain jobs? (If so, why?)

4) Would you use the service of a) a female builder, b) a female lorry driver, and c) a male childcarer?

5) How would male builders treat a new female builder?

6) How would male builders react to a woman boss?

7) Would a boss prefer men to do some jobs and women others, or would they have both sexes doing all jobs?

Children were asked about their preferred future occupations, to see whether their choices were gendered. The following questions about gender and occupation follow an original line of questioning: some are generalised, while others are very specific. By asking questions on the same theme in different ways, I expected to elicit differing responses from the children. Hence while Question Two is a very general question, Question Three aims to elicit more subtle preferences. And while questions Two and Three are both theoretical, and possibly rather remote, Question Four is specific, asking children whether they would employ non-gender-traditional workers. This question alluded to highly gender-stereotyped areas of adult work. 'Lorry driver' and 'builder' were chosen as jobs for the imaginary female worker because of their masculine images and 'childcarer' was chosen for the imaginary male worker because of its caring, feminine image.

The range of jobs children gave as their choice of future occupations are discussed first, and children's responses to the general interview questions are then examined in the order above. Children's explanations of the gender discrimination they talked about and their own constructions of gender and adult occupation are then explored.

Children's understanding of the adult workplace is necessarily limited by lack of experience. So their perceptions of it are often constructed from a combination of their own practices (e.g. conceptions of fairness, barter etc.), some experience of seeing people at work and interacting with them, and scraps of information gained from the media and adult talk, as well as imaginative theorising[1].

Children's choices of future occupation

I asked children what job they would like to do when they left school for two reasons. Firstly, although the jobs children choose at primary school age are unlikely to be their actual future occupation (see Kelly, 1989), their choices provide an indication of which jobs they feel are open to them according to gender. Secondly, previous research has found children's job choice to be extremely gender-stereotypical[2]. Dale Spender (1982) found that eight traditionally feminine jobs comprised three-quarters of the total occupations chosen by the girls in her study. This section explores whether a similar or different trend was found amongst the children in my study.

The children's job choice was extremely varied: 35 different jobs were chosen by 81 girls and 30 out of 64 boys. (See Table 1 for full list, with numbers of girls and boys who chose each job).

This question was asked during the interviews immediately after children's role-play based on adult work scenarios and some of their choices seem to have been inspired by the work roles in their plays (e.g. patient, receptionist). However, their choices remain diverse, showing a significant divergence from previous findings that girls' occupational choices were very narrow. Moreover, three of the eight most listed traditional jobs in Spender's study (air hostess, nanny, telephonist,)

Table 1: Children's Choices of Future Occupation

7 – 8 Yr. old GIRLS		7 – 8 Yr. old BOYS		10 – 11 Yr. old GIRLS		10 – 11 Yr. old BOYS	
Teacher	(8)	Policeman	(8)	Fashion Designer	(6)	Chef	(2)
Artist	(4)	Doctor	(4)	Doctor	(3)	Footballer	(2)
Nurse	(4)	Footballer	(4)	Lawyer	(3)	Sports Coach	(2)
Doctor	(3)	Fire-fighter	(3)	Teacher	(3)	Bank Manager	(1)
Barmaid	(2)	Headteacher	(3)	Performer	(2)	Business Person	(1)
Chef	(2)	Pilot	(2)	Actor	(1)	Comedian	(1)
Receptionist	(2)	Business Person	(2)	Artist	(1)	Cricketer	(1)
Shop Owner	(2)	Engineer	(2)	Civil Servant	(1)	Doctor	(1)
Writer	(2)	Hairdresser	(2)	Film Director	(1)	Engineer	(1)
Archaeologist	(1)	Life Saver	(1)	Fire Fighter	(1)	Grand Prix Driver	(1)
Baker	(1)	Movie Star	(1)	Greenpeace Activist	(1)	Graphics Designer	(1)
Ballet dancer	(1)	Petshop Worker	(1)	Newscaster	(1)	Ice Hockey Player	(1)
Banker	(1)	Sprinter	(1)	School Keeper	(1)	Mechanic	(1)
Cafe Worker	(1)	Tennis Player	(1)	Shop Owner	(1)	Pilot	(1)
Headteacher	(1)	Traveller	(1)	Vet	(1)	Something with maths	(1)
Manager	(1)	Unemployed	(1)	Work with Animals	(1)	Sprinter	(1)
Patient	(1)	World Traveller	(1)	TV Star	(1)	Don't Know	(3)
Pizza Hut Worker	(1)	Don't Know	(5)	Don't Know	(6)		
Playground Supervisor	(1)						
Vet	(1)						
Don't Know	(4)						
TOTAL:	(44)		(40)		(35)		(22)

(There was also one nine year old girl who wanted to be a scientist and one who wanted to be a housewife, and two nine year old boys who wanted to be policemen.)

were absent from girls' choices and there is a reduction in the proportions choosing other traditionally 'feminine' jobs. The methodology and age group of children in my research differs from previous studies and is therefore not directly comparable, yet the findings offer a suggestion that girls in this study see more jobs as open to them. Many of the choices are unrealistic. As I did not go on to ask whether they thought they would actually end up doing the job they had chosen, the extent to which their choices were those they expected to perform in the future is unclear. I found the girls to be generally more realistic in their choices than the boys, who often listed sporting, super-star or very unusual jobs: thirteen boys stated they wanted to become sports stars, one boy wanted to be a movie star, one a TV star and one an astronaut. The girls' choices were usually more down-to-earth, with some exceptions (for instance, fashion designer, film director, TV star). However, their choices were not unambitious: they included scientist, headteacher, solicitor and newscaster.

On the other hand, the occupational choices were quite distinct according to gender, supporting Kelly's (1989) findings that girls and boys choose different jobs. Many of the girls chose arts-based jobs (e.g. artist, writer, fashion designer, ballet dancer) or caring/public service jobs (e.g. teacher, nurse, doctor, vet). The boys more often chose sports-based occupations (e.g. footballer, sports coach, cricketer) or science and business-based jobs (e.g. engineer, bank manager, business person). This highlights an arts/caring trend in the female choices, compared to the sciences/sports trend in the male ones. So although the choices were more diverse and less stereotypical than previous studies have suggested, a binary gender dichotomy of art – female / science – male (observed by Stanworth (1981) and Whitehead (1996) in sixth form pupils' subject and career choices), still remains in the children's job choices. Also, few children chose jobs traditionally performed by the opposite sex: one girl chose scientist, one chose film director, one chose fire-fighter, and three chose solicitor. Of the boys, the only one to cross the gender barrier was the boy who chose hairdresser, suggesting that boys may be even less willing to cross occupational gender boundaries than girls[3].

More 7-8 year olds chose traditional occupations than their older counterparts (for example, eight 7-8 year old girls chose teacher and four chose nurse; and eight 7-8 year old boys chose policeman). Possibly their lesser knowledge about the variety of jobs available in the adult work market made their choice more restricted. Their choices may also be more motivated by gender stereotyping than those of the older children, if Lloyd and Duveen (1992) and Damon (1977) are right in claiming that gender role identification tends to be strongest in the earlier primary school years. Certainly this interpretation was supported by the younger girls' choices: for instance, all four choices of nurse, eight of the nine choices of teacher, and all three choices of receptionist, were made by 7-8 year old girls. It is also interesting to see also that while no 7-8 year old boys chose the job of teacher, three chose headteacher. In comparison, eight 7-8 year old girls said they wanted to become teachers and only one wanted to be a headteacher, suggesting that the public-service nature of the role was motivating them more than social status.

Children's responses to the questions about gender and occupation

The second question asked whether men and women are able to perform all jobs. Children's responses were more egalitarian than has been found in previous studies: a majority maintained that women and men could do all jobs.

Of the girls, 80% claimed both sexes have the ability to do all jobs, as did 61% of the boys. So the majority of girls gave an egalitarian response, and were supported by a smaller majority of the boys. The older children provided the most egalitarian responses (see Table 2).

The next question asked children whether they thought women or men are better at certain jobs (see Table 3). Their response to this question was more ambiguous, as over a third of both girls and boys answered that men or women are better at certain jobs and many other children said that they did not know.

A similar proportion of girls and boys said that one sex is better at certain jobs. We can assume from these responses that while the majority of children said that both sexes are able to do all jobs, many

Table 2: Do men and women have the ability to perform all jobs?

| | AGE: 7-8 | | 10-11 | |
| | girls | boys | girls | boys |
	%	%	%	%
Yes	67	45	90	76
No	19	42	0	8
Don't know and no response	14	12	10	16
N	36	33	39	25

Table 3: Are men or women better at certain jobs?

| | Girls | Boys |
	%	%
Yes	41	38
No	31	20
Don't Know and no response	28	42
N	81	64

of the children still constructed one gender or the other as more able at certain jobs. In order to examine their constructions of gender differentiation in occupation further, children were asked whether they would employ a woman builder, and/or a woman lorry driver, and/or a male childcarer, if they were in the position to do so. Children tended to give less egalitarian answers to these specific questions than they had to the generalised question about whether both genders have the ability to do all jobs (see Table 4).

Tables 4: Would children employ non-gender stereotypical workers?

i) Female lorry driver

	Girls	Boys
	%	%
Yes	64	65
No	15	20
Don't Know and no response	21	15
N	81	64

ii) Female builder

	Girls	Boys
	%	%
Yes	73	50
No	17	34
Don't know and no response	10	16
N	81	64

iii) Male childcarer

	Girls	Boys
	%	%
Yes	43	42
No	41	34
Don't know and no response	16	24
N	81	64

We can see from these tables that the response to the females being employed in male-stereotyped jobs was fairly egalitarian, with a majority of girls and boys claiming that they would employ female builders and lorry drivers (with the exception of the boys responding to the idea of a female builder, where only half said they would employ her). A slightly higher percentage of boys than girls argued that they would not employ women in these male stereotyped jobs, supporting findings of previous research that boys tend to be less egalitarian than girls regarding gender issues[4]. However, as Table 4 shows, the response to the idea of a male childcarer was far more discriminatory. Although slightly more children said they would employ a male childcarer than said they would not, the figures are much closer, and the figures for those who would employ one comprise under half the sample. So while equal opportunities ideas may be motivating children's responses regarding female ability, they are directed at women's ability to be 'like men' and not at men's ability to be 'like women'. As the tables show, a fairly large proportion of children said that they did not know whether they would employ a non-stereotypical worker, and thus did not commit themselves either way. Table 5 shows the children's responses to these questions according to age (NB the twelve children from other age-groups are not included in this analysis):

Table 5: Children who say they would employ non-gender stereotypical workers, analysed according to age

	AGE: 7-8		10-11	
	girls	boys	girls	boys
	%	%	%	%
Lorry driver	66	67	63	64
Builder	73	40	77	64
Childcarer	34	32	53	48
N	36	33	39	25

The percentage of girls and boys who were willing to employ female lorry drivers hardly varied according to age. There was little difference in willingness to employ a female builder between the girls in Year Three and Six but there was a divergence between the two male age-groups on this point. The younger boys were less egalitarian: 40% of Year Three boys said they would employ female builders compared to 64% of Year Six boys. The Year Three girls were also more discriminatory than the older girls, particularly concerning the employment of a male childcarer. There was a similar age difference in the boys' response. So these figures show again that the 7-8 year olds construct the genders more stereotypically concerning adult occupation than do the 10-11 year old group.

Children's speculations over scenarios concerning gender and adult work

This section examines children's responses concerning the fifth, sixth and seventh questions, which asked children to speculate on issues of gender in the adult workplace. Their responses show that many children construct gender as a source of discrimination in adult work and portray this discrimination as practised both by fellow employees and employers.

When asked how male builders would respond to the arrival of a woman on their team, 68% of the girls said her addition would elicit a negative response from the male builders (see Table 6). ('Positive response' includes children who argued the male builders would welcome a woman builder, 'negative response' includes children who said male builders would be hostile towards a woman builder and 'neutral response' includes children who did not think the male builders would be concerned either way.)

Table 6 shows that more girls than boys said that the builders would respond negatively. However, that nearly half the boys predicted a negative response still shows a high proportion predicting a discriminatory response from the male builders. Slightly more boys than girls maintained that the arrival of a woman builder would be met neutrally or positively on the part of the males. More boys also said that they did not know what the builders' response would be. There was little difference in response according to age.

Table 6: How would male builders treat a new female builder?

	AGE: 7-8		10-11	
	girls	boys	girls	boys
	%	%	%	%
positive response	3	6	0	4
neutral response	8	9	10	12
negative response	67	46	69	48
don't know and no response	22	39	21	36
N	36	33	39	25

Girls imagined that a male builder's reaction to a female boss would be less negative than to a female worker: 42% maintained that the gender of the boss would not matter to the builders, as did slightly more (53%) of the boys (see Table 7).

Table 7: How would male builders react to a woman boss?

	Age: 7-8		10-11	
	girls	boys	girls	boys
	%	%	%	%
positive response	3	6	3	0
neutral response	22	39	56	60
negative response	67	46	31	28
Don't know and no given response	8	9	10	12
N	36	33	39	25

However, a larger proportion of girls still thought that the builders'
reaction would be negative. There was a clear split according to age in
response to this question: only 22% of Year Three girls predicted a
neutral response to a female boss, compared to 56% of Year Six girls.
Their construction appeared to be shared by Year Six boys, as 60% of
the Year Six boys predicted a neutral reaction, compared to only 39%
of the Year Three boys.

I then asked children whether an employer would prefer to employ men
to do certain jobs and women to do others, or to have both sexes doing
all jobs (see Table 8).

*Table 8: Would a boss prefer men to do some jobs and
women others, or would they have both sexes doing all
jobs?*

	AGE: 7-8		10-11	
	girls	boys	girls	boys
	%	%	%	%
Separate jobs	25	12	33	12
The same jobs	36	33	23	40
Don't know and no response	39	55	44	48
N		36	33	39	25

This question was both general and abstract and many children did not
answer it. However, of those who did, more girls than boys argued that
an employer would allocate jobs according to gender. There was some
difference in response between the girls of different age groups. While
over a third of Year Six girls expected employers to gender differentiate, and under a quarter said gender would not affect job allocation, only a quarter of 7-8 year old girls said employers would differentiate according to gender, and over a third maintained that gender
would not be a factor in job appointment. These observations are
supported by the findings of Short and Carrington (1989), whose

sample of 6-7 year olds mainly failed to recognise that employment processes can be gender-discriminatory. Although my sample of 7-8 year olds showed greater awareness about this issue than the children in their study, it may be significant that the younger group of children in my study were a year older than the younger group in theirs. Therefore it appears that more girls in the older group constructed gender as a source of discrimination in adult occupation, perhaps because the older girls had more access to relevant information and also with greater ability to theorise. Some of the Year Three girls who predicted a negative response from male builders regarding female workers or bosses seemed to be motivated by their construction of gender relations as a 'battle of the sexes'. For example Tracy (F, 7) says of male workers' responses to a woman boss,

T: They would, I think they would all have a go at her

I: Do you think? why would [that be?

T: [Because, sort of, of, say if there was twelve people, twelve men, and one lady, the twelve men could, could hurt, hurt the one girl

I: Mm

T: Because if, if there was twelve boys and twelve girls on the other side, and there was a girl that was boss, the girls could protect their boss from the men

Tracy portrays the situation as one of 'them and us' between males and females: she actually uses the word 'sides'. As noted in the previous chapter, children of this age often appear to construct genders as in opposition in the classroom. Some girls (and boys) may project their constructions of gender in their own lives when speculating on these adult situations. In the case of employer's job allocation, however, it may seem more logical to many of the Year Three children that the employer will take on whoever is the most appropriate for the job, regardless of gender. The Year Six girls, on the other hand, may utilise their understanding of gender discrimination as a theoretical issue in order to interpret the imagined scenario and to recognise that the employer might not only be motivated by meritocratic discourses.

Discussion of children's responses to the different questions

Reviewing the responses to the interview questions, Table 9 shows the proportions of children who provided egalitarian answers to each of the questions, enabling a comparison between the different answers.

Table 9: Percentage of children whose response agreed with each statement	GIRLS	BOYS
men and women have the ability to do all jobs	80	61
neither sex is better at any job	31	20
I would employ: a female lorry driver	64	65
a female builder	73	50
a male childcarer	43	42
male builders' response to a female builder would be neutral or positive	11	16
male builders' response to a female boss would be nonchalant or positive	41	52
employers would not differentiate by gender	27	36
N	81	64

The great majority of children claimed that all jobs can be done by both sexes, not constructing the genders as different in this instance. Most children explicitly supported female ability to perform traditionally 'male' jobs (although we saw that they were less supportive of male ability to perform a traditionally female job). Greater proportions of both girls and boys stated that there are some jobs which one sex tends to perform better than the other: here more children constructed the genders as different, showing that gender remains a factor in their constructions of adult occupation. Yet in these findings children drew upon equal opportunities discourses in their responses more than in previous studies. Previous research showed children assigning nearly all adult jobs to one gender or the other, whereas the great majority of children in my study said that both genders can do all jobs and many said they would employ non-stereotypical workers. It may be that equal opportunities discourses have become more available in school in recent times, but I suggest that this difference in findings may also be due to my methods and the way my questions were presented. The context of an individual interview with an adult, female interviewer in an educational environment may have encouraged children to draw upon equity discourses, yet the majority of the studies discussed above were also conducted by women in an educational environment. So in my view the format of the questions had the biggest impact in eliciting more egalitarian constructions about gender and occupation, besides greater access to equal opportunities discourse.

This is supported by the different responses given when the questions were framed differently. We can see from Table 9 that the specific questions elicited different responses to the generalised, theoretical question inquiring whether men and women are able to do the same jobs. Moreover, the difference in responses concerning children's own constructions (i.e. whether they would employ non-stereotypical workers) and those concerning the actions of others in the adult workplace, shows that children construct gender as a source of discrimination in adult work. In real life they apparently consider that a female builder would not be welcomed by male fellows and that many employers would differentiate in job allocation.

Children's explanations about their construction of gender as a source of discrimination in work

The explanations children offered for their responses are now investigated. Noting a change in teachers' discourses regarding girls' future careers, Kenway *et al* (1994) and Skelton (1997a) argue that teachers have become more aware of equal opportunities issues. In my study, Pavlos (M, 9) reports that teachers in his school tell people off if they make sexist comments and many children appear to recognise that any sexist statements may be met with disapproval from adults in a school environment. Therefore, rather than risking being seen as sexist themselves, children may attempt to rationalise their discriminatory constructions through other explanations. Billig *et al* (1988) have observed such processes of disguising reactionary discourse by arguing a reactionary view in a 'rational' manner. They argue that dominant discourses of democratic justice and liberalism position discriminatory discourse as reactionary and uncivilised. Therefore, people wishing to discriminate often try to explain their views in 'rational' ways. To illustrate this, they cite racists who begin sentences with the phrase, 'I'm not racist but...', and then justify their discriminatory stance with reasoning such as 'black people don't like whites', rather than with white supremicist arguments. In the following sections I show that children often attempted to rationalise gender discrimination in a similar way. However, it should be remembered that I was *asking* children to explain their constructions and so may have elicited such responses where they would not otherwise have been provided. Even so, a minority of children did give discriminatory answers without trying to justify them – I suggest that these children may not yet be aware that these might meet disapproval from adults.

The ability of both sexes to do all jobs

Only a small minority of mainly younger children argued that both sexes did *not* have the ability to do all jobs. Many of these children simply based their explanations on the principle that 'men's jobs' are for men and 'women's jobs' are for women. Thus Lesley (F, 7) responds to the question of whether men and women can do the same jobs: '(.) Not a doctor they can't; cos that's for boys – only nurses they can', and about men wanting to be nurses she says, 'Yeah (.) but they train as doctors first, they can't be nurses – thassa *woman's* job'. She goes on to argue that women can do any jobs they wish, 'Unless it's a men's job', and that although women can drive cars, they cannot be lorry drivers: 'S'like it's a *men's* job, so they wouldn't'. Similarly, Shamin (F, 7) explains that she would not employ a male childminder, 'Because ladies, ladies have to keep the child, and mans have to do the building work' and Rafic (M, 9) asserts that women cannot be pilots 'because, it's not a, really job for a *girl*. Like, girls are, girls are not supposed to do what, er, *boys* do'. He continues, 'Like, they're better at doing jobs like, women are better at doing jobs like going out shopping and doing the housework, and men should go to *work*'. Children were a small but vocal minority who did not appear to draw on equity discourses at all. Their open presentation of these rigid, traditionally discriminatory constructions was strikingly different to the rest of the children: most children appeared wary of vocalising discriminatory statements in my presence and usually attempted to rationalise these through other arguments. Yet children in this small group were apparently unconcerned about any stigma attached to gender discriminatory discourse, openly asserting discriminatory views, seemingly without expecting challenge or disapproval. None of these children came from the oldest class. Gender category maintenance discourses may be more important for children in the 7-8 year old age-group and may outweigh equity discourses.

Some of the children who said men and women *can* do the same jobs expressed aggrievement that others do not share their views. For example, Rebecca (F, 8) complains about discrimination when she explains to me that men as well as women can be professional ballet dancers, but that women cannot be professional football players:

R: I know sometimes it's not fair, because girls can't play football, but boys can do ballet (.) it's not *fair*

I: Mm

R: So, I think they should do a new law that girls can play football, because I'm good at football

I: Yeah, they can play football here can't they?

R: Yeah, but in real life they can't

I: [Yeah

R: [I can play football good, I can beat my friend, Leon, and 'e's a *really* good one, 'e says 'e's a professional, but 'e's not really

Rebecca's frustration at what she perceives as an unjust situation is evident, but she offers a constructive suggestion ('a new law') to right the situation. Likewise, Emily (F, 10) describes how she challenges the boys' sexist assumptions on this subject:

E: Well like the boys, some of the boys in our class um, they're always saying 'oh when I grow up I'm gonna be a, stuff, when we're a bit younger we saying 'when I grow up I'm gonna be such and such, and we said 'oh I'd like to be that' they'd say {high and mighty voice} No, ladies can't be that, they're not strong enough

I: Really? how does that make you feel?

E: Well, well I feel (.) um I feel that everyone's equal and you should all, if even if you don't think you're good at it you should have a try and things like that

I: Yes (.) so what did you used to say to the boys when they said things like that?

E: I said we're all equal and we can erm, can do all things, cos we're all good at some things

Why men or women are better at certain jobs

In their more frequent assertations that men or women are better at particular jobs, children used many different arguments to justify their statements in the light of my questions. For instance, Naomi (F, 11) explains her reasons for feeling that men make superior chiropodists and doctors and women better nurses:

I: Are there any that men are better at or that women are better at? (.) or do you think they're all the same generally?

N: Um, um (.) I mean some things I've never seen men, I mean *ladies* do

I: Mm like what?

N: Um, a chiropodist I've never seen a lady   [chiropodist

I: [Oh really?

N: Cos I had to go to a man, and (.)

I: Mm (.) but do you think she could if she wanted to or not?

N: (.) Probably but, men seem to be nicer at that sort of thing

I: Oh really?

N: Yeh

I: Wh- in what way?

N: Well I, they're, they explain everything as they go along and they're really kind=

I: Oh right, right that's interesting yeh

N: But I think, that doctors are better as ladies (.) no I think *doctors* are better as men and *nurses* are better as *ladies*

I: Oh really? why's that?

N: {laughs} I don't know (.) I ...

I: W- what makes a man better as a doctor and a woman better as a nurse?

N: Well (.) um, men lose their tempers, um much easier, sometimes, and are more (.) because you lose your temper easily, more easily as a nurse

I: Oh how, why's that?

N: Well, cos if you're a nurse like, you have to do more things in the hospital and stuff

I: Right yeh

N: Than if you're a doctor

Naomi's claim that men make superior chiropodists is based upon her own experience (her chiropodist, whom she likes, is male and she has never seen a female chiropodist), yet this explanation still gender differentiates, as she assumes that the sexes will perform the job differently. Naomi argues that women can keep their temper under stress better than men and so are more suited to the very stressful role of nurse. But Shamin (F, 7) maintains that women are more suited to nursing (and men to medicine) because women are prone to error: while they can manage with the easier role of nurse they cannot cope with the demanding position of doctor:

I: Why are men better at those jobs then, do you think?

S: Cos, you know doctors, they could do any (2) they could work really hard at- (.) ladies can't do too much, woman can't do too much

I: Why's that then, why do you think that is?

S: Umm, man could do like, someone had an operation, they could give injections or something, and, or do the heart problem; they could do that, and the ladies could do the erm- just injections

I: Right (.) why do you think the women wouldn't be so good at the complicated operations?

S: Cos, maybe they'd get it wrong

So Shamin presents an opposite argument to Naomi's, concerning the same occupation. In these cases I suggest that the children are simply attempting to justify their stereotypical statements regarding the gender of doctors and nurses (or other jobs) with any arguments they can think of.

Why children would or would not employ non-stereotypical workers

Children's explanations of their own gender discrimination in refusing to employ non-stereotypical workers often involved similar attempts at rationalisation. Such processes are evident when Diva (F, 10) is forced to change her argument in the face of my questions. When I ask her why she would prefer not to employ women builders she replies:

D: Because, you know, they haven't got the same kind of hands, they're not, they might, they probably might just go down {gestures down}

I: Do you think?

D: Yeah

I: So you think a man would be better at being a builder?

D: Yeah (.) because you've got to like, stick everything on, and, get all the pieces to do it

I: Mm, how come a woman wouldn't be able to do that then?

D: Because they haven't got, precious hands

I: Right, say a woman like, did have really big hands or whatever, and she really wanted to be a builder, do you think she could then?

D: No:o

I: No? How come?

D: Because, it's too- (.) I don't know (.) it's too, they won't be enough, careful enough

I: Mm

D: They wouldn't take care

Her initial claim is that women do not have the right hands needed for building work. However, when I present her with the possibility of women with suitable hands, Diva resorts to a different argument, that women are not careful enough to be builders. As one argument is countered she abandons it and selects another to justify her rejection of female builders. Children often went to extraordinary lengths in attempts to justify their views with practical, rather than blatantly discriminatory, explanations. Andrew (M, 7) argues that his objection to employing women builders is due to the possibility of their making mistakes when flicking their long hair back, while Tracy (F, 7) claims to object to them because they would not buy the correct hard hats. She opposes the idea of women lorry drivers because they might not be so good at jumping out of the lorry cab window in the event of a crash!

The majority of reasons given for not employing non-gender-stereotypical workers followed similar themes: children argued that women would not be strong enough to be proficient builders and lorry drivers and that women are 'better' with children than men. Both these strains of argument are based upon essentialist foundations, the assumption that women and men are 'naturally' suited to different things. Illustrating this point, Kelly (F, 11) claims she would not employ female builders: 'Um (.) no I'd get men cos like they're sort – they're quite *strong*, m, a bit stronger than, women, and they'd do it a bit quicker'. Charis (F, 7) argues she would not employ women lorry drivers, 'because erm they're too heavy for erm women to drive, and it, erm, all the steering's hard'. Rafic (M, 9) explains why he would prefer a female childcarer: 'Um, because women know *more* about, um, they can take care because they know the *feeling* of the baby' and Annalea (F, 7) explains that she would not employ a male childcarer in the following way:

I: =would you employ a man childcarer to look after your [baby?

A: [No

I: No, why not?

A: Cos they can't look after babies

I: No why not though?

A: (.) Cos- (2)

I: Why is a woman better?

A: (.) Cos they know about babies

I: Mm (.) why do they know more do you think?

A: Because they've got them

I: Right (.) what if a man had looked after a baby while his wife went to work, would he know enough or=

A: No

I: He still wouldn't

A: No

Many children appeared to feel that such essentialism is a legitimate and accepted discourse and so a valid explanation for gender discrimination. In their case study observing a class discussion of sex roles, Baker and Davies (1989) found that the teacher used similar essentialist arguments to explain differences between gender roles. Essentialism was applied particularly to childcare: most children in the large group who claimed they would prefer a female childcarer alluded to female nurturing qualities, noted that men were not used to looking after children and hinted that women are 'naturally' more able with children.

When I continued to question their arguments, the children usually abandoned their claims to rationality in favour of reactionary assertions. For example, as Andrew (M, 7) has justified rejecting women builders because they would make mistakes while pushing back their hair, I ask him:

I: Oh I see what if they had short hair?

A: (.) {intake of breath} Like, then they'll *slip*

I: (.) Mm, why would they slip more than a man though?

A: No they'll slip and then their hands would go {gestures} an' then they push 'em down and=

I: Why, why would they do that more than a man though?

A: (.) Because men are *better* than girls when they do houses

I: Mm, why though?

A: I don't know

Likewise, Shofic (M, L, 7) argues that women are not tall enough to be lorry drivers:

I: So you'd only have tall men would it   [be?

S: [Yeh

I: What if there were some really tall women, cos like, models are really tall,

    they're about six foot- what if they wanted a job, would you give them one?

S: *No*

I: How come?

S: (.) *Mad*

I: Mm? (.) bad? what, who's bad?

S: The lady, the people who want to come

I: Okay, you don't think they'd be good?

S: No

I: But I thought you said women and men can do all the same jobs?

S: Yeh

I: But not- but you wouldn't employ them

S: No

These extracts are alike in that both children try to justify their gender-discriminatory stance through 'rational' argument yet when they are forced to abandon these they conclude by asserting discriminatory arguments. The 'rational' arguments they drew upon were gender-discriminatory notions of female physical inferiority and stereotypical gender characteristics, which attempt to justify gender discrimination *through* sexism. However, these children did not capitulate to an equity view under the logic of my questioning but instead reasserted their sexist stance despite their forced abandonment of rationality discourse. So failure of these arguments did not necessarily lead to a rejection of the gender construction.

The female builder

Table 6 shows that more boys than girls spoke of a neutral or even a positive response from the male builders to a female work-mate. Patrick (M, 7) goes so far as to state about the male builders: '(.) I would think (.) they would be quite happy 'cos they (.) got a rare person on their building team'. This optimistic view could be due to lesser awareness of gender discrimination compared to the girls (because females are more often on the receiving end of sexism they may be more politicised about this issue), or possibly male sympathy prompts the boys to portray the male builders in a more egalitarian light. Billig *et al* (1988) have suggested that Western democratic discourses of individual rights position power advantages as totalitarian and that this leads people to deny recognition of their own power advantages. Such a denial of power could explain the boys' lesser construction of gender as a source of discrimination (and thus male power) in adult occupation.

Of the children who suggested a negative response on the part of male builders, more boys than girls claimed that this would be justified because of the incompetence or inappropriateness of a female for the job (six of the 28 boys who provided an explanation, compared to only one of the 44 girls who did so). Thus we see that a number of boys continue to construct gender as different concerning adult occupation. The majority of both girls and boys (22 of the 28 boys and 37 of the 44 girls) maintained that the male builders' negative reaction would be due to male perceptions of women as weak, leading them to ridicule and ostracise the woman, presuming her to be physically incompetent. Other explanations included those of two boys and two girls who said that the male builders would be jealous of the woman because women 'make prettier buildings' and because of her muscles and appearance. Three girls claimed that male builders would assume that women are too feminine for such work and should be doing the housework instead. A minority of the children (one boy and two girls) explained their expectations of the male builders' reactions in relation to wider issues of gender discrimination. For instance, Angela (F, 7) demonstrates her realisation that the world of adult occupation can be discriminatory:

I: What do you think the men builders would say about the woman builder?

CHILDREN'S TALK ABOUT GENDER AND ADULT WORK • **73**

A: Um, well, I think they would just go into a fight with her say I don't know why we've got a woman builder cos they're not stronger than men

I: Mm (.) and would they be right or not?

A: (2) I don't really know

I: No:o, what would the woman have to do?

A: Nothing because, she wouldn't even know

I: Right right I see, so they'd just gossip behind her back would they?

A: Yeah and, mm, if there was a weak man, they would still be saying it when the lady would be stronger

From her final comment we can see that Angela has perceived the irrationality of gender discrimination. Likewise Rebecca (F, 8) explains that she would feel hesitant about allowing a female builder to build her house, because although she said that women and men should be allowed to do the same things, she feels that a woman might not be qualified; and her reply here draws on a view of the adult world as skewed against women:

I: Mm, do you think if the woman was qualified you'd let her do it?

R: Yeh

I: Yeah, okay (.) why do you think that women wouldn't be so qualified as men?

R: Cos people don't let 'em do it

So a substantial proportion of the children who envisaged the male builders responding negatively to the appointment of a female builder constructed gender as a potential source of discrimination in adult occupation. And of these the majority of girls, as well as a large group of boys, said that they disagreed with this situation. For example, Natasha (F, 10) argues that the male builders would think the woman builder incapable of the job, and I ask her why she imagines they would believe this:

N: I don't know, because I suppose, they all think men are stronger than women, but I don't think that

I: What do you think women would have to do, I mean, to deal with it?

N: (.) Just show them she's any, she's as good as them

I: Right, right (.) do you think that sort of thing will change, or do you think it'll always be like that?

N: It'll always be like that

Natasha's talk suggests an acknowledgement that women face a constant struggle against gender discriminatory prejudices and that she does not envisage these prejudices lessening but appears to accept them as a fact of life. Leke (M, 7), however, suggests a practical solution to sexism on the building site, proposing to sack sexist builders and employ women in their place to support the original female:

I: Yeah, say you had all men working there apart from one woman (.) what do you think the men would think of her?

L: (.) That she can't work properly

I: Mm, why would they think that?

L: And then, if anyone says that I would ki- chop them out and get a new lady

I: Right

L: So they could hang around together

The female boss

Of the children who envisaged a negative reaction to a female boss on the part of the male builders, regardless of her higher occupational status, a tiny minority of boys (two) explained this as a reasonable response, because women would be incompetent in such a role. However, the rest of the children said rather that there would be a hostile response from the men either because of male gender discrimination or because of general hostility between the sexes. Children who argued that hostility towards a woman boss would be due to male discrimination explained this as manifesting in the builders' perceptions of a female boss as 'soft', 'weak' and incompetent. For example, Richard (M, 10) maintains that the men would say 'she doesn't have enough sense, to work'; Simone (M, 7) explains, 'You know! (.) some boys think girls are softies'; and Patrick (M, 7) agrees that the men would think it 'silly' having a woman boss.

However, Table 7 shows that, compared to their predictions of a negative response to a female builder, a greater number of older children predicted a neutral or positive response to a female boss on the part of the male builders. This suggests that they may construct power derived from status as able to override power derived from gender. For example, where Angela (F, 7) argued previously that a female builder would be victimised by her male fellows, she claims that a female boss would face no such difficulties, as the men would be forced to flatter her for fear of being 'thrown out'. Likewise Kasheef (M, 10) argues that male builders might not like the prospect of taking orders from a female but that they 'would have to put up with it' because, he concludes, 'a boss is a boss'. This interpretation is voiced by the majority of children. Although a substantial proportion anticipate no conflict at all, most envisage the men concealing their sexism for practical reasons, in view of the woman's higher occupational status. As Karen (F, 10) points out, '(.) Well, they probably, they might respect her in case they lose their jobs'. Power was understood as the key issue and these children appeared to recognise the conflict between two different power dichotomies at work in the scenario – male/female, and boss/ workers. Status was not always interpreted as outweighing gender in the power balance: for example, Patrick (M, 7) maintains that a female fellow worker would simply be viewed as a novelty by the males, but that a female boss giving them orders would be unacceptable to them. The conflict in power dichotomy is nevertheless recognised both by children who envisaged gender as outweighing status in terms of power and those who envisaged the reverse. This shows children's acknowledgement that status can be re-written depending on the environment and the power relationships within it.

Job allocation

In response to the question 'would a boss prefer men to do some jobs and women to do others, or would they have both sexes doing all jobs?', far more girls than boys expected employers to discriminate according to gender. Again the boys (particularly the older ones) present themselves as believers that the adult work place is based on a meritocratic system, suggesting a denial of gender discrimination and the connotations of male advantage associated with it. Joseph (M, 11) illustrates this point:

I: Do you think that they'd {*employers*} want women to do certain jobs and men to do different jobs, or do you think they'd let them have a mixture?

J: I'd give 'em a chance on a mixture (.) I, I, I think they'd probably give 'em a chance on a mixture, but not many people do that

I: No (.) why do you think it is that in real life sort of, most secretaries and receptionists are women, and most builders and so on are men?

J: Ermm, I don't really think that's a bad thing, because um (.) well (.) builders have to lift very very heavy things

I: Mm

J: I'm not being sexist or anything, but it can be very heavy

I: Yes (.) so do you think that most women- some women would be strong enough but some wouldn't?

J: Mm, some wouldn't

I: Yeah, yes (.) so you think they're physically suited, men are physically suited to be builders?

J: (.) Yeah, some of 'em (.) but I've seen loads of women builders who're really big and strong

I: Yes, yes there are a lot of strong women aren't there?

J: Yeh

Joseph is eager to distance himself from any discrimination but suggests the lack of women builders is due to practical reasons. However he then realises that this argument could be understood as sexist, so quickly qualifies that he has, 'seen loads of women builders who're *really* big and strong'. I suggest this qualification aims to demonstrate his open-minded and non-generalising attitude. Of course, though his having seen 'loads' of women builders seems unlikely, this claim contradicts his original argument that there are few women builders because it is such heavy work.

The children who argued that employers *do* differentiate by gender when allocating jobs fell into two distinct categories: those who assumed that an employer would employ men in different jobs from women for practical reasons and a larger group comprising those who maintained that employers would differentiate by gender due to their gender discriminatory attitudes. Of the former, the vast majority claimed that gender-stereotypical job allocation is appropriate in light of the different attributes of the sexes. They therefore assumed that employers would perceive the issue in the same manner. A small number of Year Three children offered other practical reasons: for instance, that it would be impractical to have men and women working together, as husband and wife could then work together and would distract each other; or that there might be conflict between genders.

A larger group of children argued that employers would differentiate due to their gender discriminatory attitudes. Their responses ranged from those who said they thought an employer (often assumed to be male) would think men and women should do traditional jobs but were unable to explain why, to children (usually girls) who presented their response within a wider argument about gender discrimination. When Claudia (F, 10) claims that men and women can do all jobs and I ask whether they actually do, she answers:

C: No (.) *Yeah*, but mostly the men- like, the *managers* choose them to be like *maids* and stuff, and mostly chauffeurs, and things like that

I: Mm (.) why do you think that is?

C: Cos they think it's man's job to be chauffeurs

I: Right (.) but you disagree?

C: Yeh

Karen (F, 10) clarifies and concludes this perspective aptly in the following extract:

I: Would they want women to do certain jobs and men to do different jobs, or would they have a mixture?

K: *I'd* have a mixture

I: Mm, what do you think happens in real life?

K: They'd probably have women doing certain jobs and men doing different jobs

I: Mm, why do you reckon that is?

K: Sexist

Hence many children, particularly older girls, appear sharply aware of gender discrimination as potentially damaging to women's prospects in the adult workplace: their familiarity with and understanding of the debate over gender discrimination is drawn on when discussing situations outside their own immediate experience (i.e. adult occupation).

Summary

To recap, these findings about children's choice of future occupation show that female job choice is quite diverse and that many girls chose powerful, high-status jobs. However, a binary gender dichotomy still exists between the *type* or *attributes* of jobs chosen by girls and boys and few children chose jobs which are traditionally performed by the opposite sex. When examining children's responses to my questions concerning gender and adult work, I found that the majority stated that men and women can do the same jobs and most supported this view even when questioned about the most gender-stereotypical occupations. Thus many children constructed the genders as *not* different regarding adult occupation. However, the concept of equal opportunities appeared to be more often applied to women than to men (fewer children said that they would employ a male childcarer than women builders and lorry drivers). And gender-discriminatory constructs were evident in many children's responses, with a majority of children claiming that men or women are *better* at certain jobs. I found that more boys predicted egalitarian behaviour from employers and male fellow workers: girls more often predicted discrimination from both sources.

Turning to the constructions of gender and adult occupation underlying the children's responses, my figures confirm the findings of previous studies suggesting that girls tend to express more egalitarian views than boys. They also show that the 10-11 year old children gender-discriminate less than their 7-8 year old counterparts. This does not necessarily confirm that children of this age are 'naturally' less egalitarian (as implied by developmental psychology studies); two other factors might contribute to the younger children's more stereotypical expressions. These are: stronger gender category maintenance (which will lessen as children become more confident about their gender identities) and a lesser awareness of equal opportunities discourse.

Many children attempted to rationalise their discriminatory constructions and there was great diversity in their explanations. However,
essentialist constructions (e.g. that men are naturally more suited to
manual work and women to childcare) were often used to demonstrate
the rationality of gender discrimination in adult occupation. Children
of both genders, but particularly girls, constructed gender as a source
of discrimination in the adult workplace. Certainly the majority of
children could apply their knowledge of gender issues to scenarios
beyond their immediate experience. Moreover, awareness appeared
widespread that gender discrimination is an issue of power: many
children (again, particularly girls) maintained that power derived from
higher status would outweigh power derived from gender. There was a
broad diversity of response concerning the acceptability or unaccept-
ability of gender discrimination in the adult workplace. Similarly,
children drew on a diversity of ideas when discussing the issue. However, the large majority of girls and over half the boys articulated concepts of equity and fairness to declare disapproval of gender discrimination in adult occupation.

Notes

1. For a discussion of children's ideas about adult work and the extent of their economic
    understanding, see Hutchings (1990, 1995), Ross (1990, 1992) and Berti and Bombi,
    (1988).

2. Holland and Skouras (1979), Spender (1982), and Sharpe (1976) examined the job choices
    of adolescent secondary school girls and found them to be highly stereotypical. Research on
    primary school children's occupational choice by Robb (1981) and Adams and Walkerdine
    (1986) drew similar conclusions.

3) See also the work of Whitehead (1996) and Lightbody and Durndell (1996), who found
    secondary school boys more likely to choose gender-stereotypical jobs than their female
    counter-parts.

4) Smithers (1984), Lindholm (1978), Furnham and Stacey (1991) and Taylor (1986) found
    that boys' opinions regarding equal opportunity were less egalitarian than those of girls.

CHAPTER 4

CHILDREN'S CONSTRUCTIONS OF SEXISM IN SCHOOL

This chapter examines children's discussions of sexism in their school lives and their reports of the strategies they employ to cope with or resist it. It represents an attempt to 'ground' discourse analysis in an investigation of the social implications of gender discourse. As noted in the first chapter, many feminists have voiced concern at post-structuralist analyses' lack of engagement with social reality and the power differences in our society. In keeping with my 'post-modern-modern' approach, the little researched question of whether or not children constructed gender as a source of unfair discrimination is investigated.

By 'sexism' I mean any verbal or physical manifestation of the assumption that one sex is superior to the other. This includes, then, assumptions that one gender is inadequate, the practice of unfair gender discrimination based on this assumption, and physical or verbal abuse on the basis of gender.

There has been other research on sexism in school. For instance, investigating the sexism of secondary school pupils, Herbert (1989), Lees (1993) and Larkin (1994) show how girls suffer both verbal and physical abuse at the hands of boys and sometimes male teachers. Herbert argues that such behaviour on the part of the boys is often ignored or trivialised by teachers, who claim that it is 'natural' behaviour, thus legitimising it further. This finding is echoed by Skelton's (1997b) research on hegemonic masculinity among primary school boys, where she found harassment of girls by boys being dismissed as 'routine naughtiness' by teachers. Both Herbert and Lees argue that this sexist abuse functions as a control to regulate girls' behaviour.

There have been few studies of sexism among pupils in the primary school, however. Skelton's study is unique in her rigorous analysis of boys' heterosexual harassment of girls in the primary school. My research differs from hers in that her method was observation, whereas I questioned children overtly about sexism among pupils. The approaches have different strengths and weaknesses: Skelton was able to observe incidents herself first hand, but did not ask children about their experiences. Whereas my interviews probed the children's own constructions of sexism and sexist incidents, but did not observe such incidents actually occurring.

A few other studies have touched upon such issues in the primary school. Walkerdine (1981) reports an instance where young boys draw on sexist discourse to position themselves powerfully in relation to their female teacher: the boys position the teacher as powerless by referring to her in sexist terms, constructing their power as males as more salient than her power as a teacher. The incident begins when a boy challenges a female classmate with an abusive reference to female genitalia: 'You're a stupid cunt, Annie' (p.4). The teacher rebukes the boy, who then turns his sexist abuse in her direction. It is the confrontation between boys and teacher which is focused on by Walkerdine, rather than that between the boy and girl.

In their study of racism in the lives of primary school children, Troyna and Hatcher (1992) also observe 'aggressive verbal and physical behaviour by some, though not all, of the boys, both among themselves and directed at the girls' (p.54), and report that many of the girls in their study talked in their interviews about harassment and name-calling by boys. Troyna and Hatcher say they did not observe boys using 'sexist terms', but do not define what these might be. While this 'aggressive verbal and physical behaviour' on the part of the boys is explained in terms of the construction and maintenance of gender identities, an analysis is not developed because the study's specific focus is on children's talk about racism. Short (1993) interviewed children concerning gender stereotypical roles and found that many children rejected traditional stereotypes but still participated in gender-discriminatory behaviour in the classroom. However, the nature and extent of such gender discrimination are not fully discussed. I seek here to provide a more focused analysis of primary school children's construction of sexism in school.

When moving on to the subject of sexism in children's lives during the interview, I first asked children,

> Do you know what the word 'sexism' means?

This question aimed to discover how many children could give a definition of the word 'sexism' which specified gender-discrimination or the idea that one sex claims to be superior to the other. I wanted to find out how many understood the concept, before analysing their reports of discrimination in school. Short and Carrington (1989) suggest that young children have little understanding of sexism, as they did not recognise the existence of sexism in the adult workplace. I sought to discover whether the children would be able to talk about sexism in their own lives.

The question children were asked concerning sexism in their school lives was:

> Do boys ever pick on girls just because they're girls, or girls pick on boys just because they're boys? (If they had previously provided an appropriate definition of 'sexism' or used the word in their discussion, I merely asked whether sexism occurs in school.)

This question deliberately did not use the actual word 'sexism', so that those children who did not understand the word could still discuss the issue. Obviously the phrase 'pick on' and the word 'sexism' are emotive and this negative imagery will inevitably impact on children's constructions. However, I was unable to come up with a more neutral phrase which implied the same thing.

Children's understanding of 'sexism' and reports of its occurrence in school

Table 1 shows how children's understanding of the word 'sexism' varied greatly according to age. ('Relevant example' refers to children who provided an example of sexist behaviour – e.g. 'It's like when boys

Table 1: Children's responses to the question, 'do you know what the word 'sexism' means?'

AGE:	7-8		10-11	
	girls	boys	girls	boys
	%	%	%	%
Appropriate definition (possibly with example)	6	3	56	52
Relevant Example Only	3	6	3	12
Don't Know (or inappropriate definition)	83	82	31	28
No Answer Given	8	9	10	8
N	36	33	39	25

don't let the girls play football', rather than a reasonable definition of sexism.)

These figures support Short and Carrington's (1989) finding that younger children have little understanding of the word sexism: only a small percentage of 7-8 year old girls and boys in my study gave definitions based on the idea of discrimination against persons because of their gender. A few children in this age group provided an example as an explanation, but the overwhelming majority did not give an appropriate answer. Most of these children said they did not know, while a small number confused 'sexism' with 'sex', and gave answers either concerning biological gender or sexual activity. However, the responses of the 10-11 year old group showed a very different picture: 54% of girls and boys provided an appropriate definition of sexism, and a further 8% gave relevant examples instead of a definition. The figures depict a similar level of understanding of the word sexism between boys and girls in each age group. Thus the older children generally had a greater understanding of the meaning of the word than did their younger counterparts and there was little difference in understanding according to gender.

Being able to provide a definition of sexism as gender discrimination indicates some understanding of the concept. I found that the majority of the younger children could give examples of sexism when asked whether girls pick on boys simply because they are boys and vice-versa, yet most said they did not know what the word sexism meant.

I had expected that the older children's greater understanding of sexism would lead to greater awareness of the issue and therefore to higher numbers of 10-11 year olds claiming to observe sexist incidents in school. But in fact the figures are very similar: about 80% of girls and 60% of boys in both age groups maintained that they observed incidents of gender discrimination or antagonism between children in schools (see Table 2).

Table 2: 'Do girls pick on boys just because they're boys, or boys pick on girls just because they're girls, in school?'				
AGE:	7-8		10-11	
	Girls	Boys	Girls	Boys
	%	%	%	%
Yes	81	58	79	60
No	6	30	13	20
Don't Know and No response	14	12	8	20
N	36	33	39	25

So the majority of children constructed gender as a source of discrimination in their schools. The large proportion of children claiming they observe instances of sexism in school, compared to the smaller number of those who could define the meaning of sexism, suggests that many children may not yet be able to label such experiences as sexist.

Of those children who said that they observe instances of pupil sexism in school, 80% of girls gave examples of sexist incidents in which they were on the receiving end either specifically or collectively (e.g. 'Oh, the boys always make fun of the girls'). The remaining 20% gave examples of things which had happened to females other than themselves, whereas only one boy claimed that girls in his class were sexist against him. This could be due to 'macho' discourses which construct such complaints of victimisation as unacceptable for boys, yet there were several complaints from boys concerning racism and bullying. The children's accounts give a picture of primary school in which sexism between pupils occurs frequently and where it is almost exclusively practised by boys, against girls.

However, some children said that boys do not pick on girls or vice versa, and thus did not construct gender as a source of discrimination in school. Table 2 shows that rather more boys than girls said that sexism did not occur. There are three possible explanations for this. Firstly, the boys may be less aware of the issue because they are not the target of gender-discrimination. Secondly, the girls could have exaggerated the extent of sexist incident between pupils. Or, lastly, the boys might be trying to portray society as non-gender-discriminatory because they wish to disassociate themselves from sexism and patriarchal power. In his analysis of modern masculinity, Middleton (1992) observes people's tendency to avoid focusing on their power advantages and in the last chapter we noted Billig's *et al* (1988) argument that Western culture's strong discourses of egality and democracy make people embarrassed by power – and that power is thus disguised or denied. Such denial of power advantage could explain the boys' lesser construction of gender as a source of discrimination.

Children's accounts of the different types of sexism experienced in school

In this section the types of sexism reported by children are categorised and discussed.

Verbal abuse

Male derision of things female is often reflected in the verbal insults girls frequently reported receiving from boys. Reema (F, 9) describes how boys often make fun of girls' hair and clothes and Chantelle (F, 7) informs me that the boys call the girls 'stupid names'. When I ask her what the girls' response to this is, Chantelle replies:

C: We argue back, but they always seem to win

I: Aww, why?

C: They've got more cusses

Her explanation echoes the findings of Lees (1993), who demonstrates that girls are severely restricted in their ability to chastise boys by the lack of vocabulary of insults relating to masculinity: the massive majority of such words denote femininity. In response to my question of whether she experiences sexism from the boys, Sharma (F, 11) explains how the boys call her names and cannot accept similar action by a girl:

S: Well, I have to say, they [boys] do say that to me (.) they say Oh go away you big nose, or Go away, I don't wanna sit with a girl

I: Mm

S: Because when I'm speaking to Claudine, they butt in (.) so I say Oh why can't I do the same thing, I mean, they do it to me so I do it to them, and they say Oh go away, we don't wanna play with no girls, and stop ....

I: So they don't like it when you act the same way they do, is it?

S: Mm, yeh

Chantelle and Sharma are clear about the difficulty they have in retaliating in the face of the boys' verbal abuse.

Teasing

A major source of complaint from the girls (and often reported by boys, though none admitted to participating in such behaviour), was male teasing, based on claims of female inadequacy. For instance, Tracy (F, 7) claims that boys tease girls 'because they think they're more tougher', and Matthew (M, 11) reports that one boy told girls that, 'men have got real muscles and ladies have got paper muscles'. Besides these claims of female inadequacy, a second type of sexist teasing commonly described by children involved open ridicule and disdain of things female, simply because of their being female or having female associations. Thus Rebecca (F, 8) explains that she would like the boys to join in with the games she plays with her girlfriends but that they won't: 'they don't want to, say It's too girly-girly-girly'. Similarly, during their role-play Mike (M, 8) asserts that Tanvier (M, 7) should play the part of nurse 'because he's a girl'. Mike goes on to tell me in his interview that Tanvier is 'a poofter' because, 'he hits girls and girls hit him', suggesting that Tanvier's masculinity is revoked by participating in brawls with girls (whom Mike declares 'wimps': obviously the words 'wimp' and 'poofter' themselves imply a lack of masculinity).

Physical abuse

While the former types of sexism were verbal, the third type of sexist incident described by children was physical. I have given rather more space to quotes from this category than to the other expressions of sexism, because I was surprised at the extent of girls' portrayal of themselves as on the receiving end of male violence. Incidents of male violence against girls were reported frequently in all the schools except Lady Mary, and several girls claimed that they themselves had been on the receiving end. For example, Lesley (F, 7) describes:

L: Once I got beat by Johnnie Lipton cos, 'e had this yellow paper, I put it back, I took it from him, nearly, and 'e just punched me in the belly, an' I was crying on the floor, and then he grabbed a chair and nearly threw it at me, but I stopped it

I: Just because you stood up for yourself? that's awful isn't it? and does that sort of thing happen a lot? (.) {she nods} yeah?

L: He bullies a lot of girls

Claudine (F, 7) reports that when she refused to let a boy join in her game, he responded in the following way:

C: =And then he came and just banged my head on the wall, then I told Miss and then he *punched* me in front of them, and I had to go to Miss Locker, and then he said I punched him

I: Oh that's terrible

C: And I didn't

Annette (F, 7) describes:

A: (.) They [boys], sometimes they push me on the floor an' I tell them off, some, …, or someone, told, told them off and (.) we tell it to Miss Lewis

I: Right, why do they push you on the floor?

A: Because they don't like girls

Michael (M, 7) informs me:

M: Well, it's *mostly* boys that tease the girls, cos um (.) some of the boys, right, get into a group, make up a plan, and then start, start going up to the girls, throwing basketballs at them=

I: Do they?

M: Yeh, kick footballs at them,   [and, going, coming up to them and like, you know when um, sometimes when=

I: [Oh *dear*

M: =they get into groups, put hands over s-, s- {gestures}

I: Mm (.) shoulders?

M: The boys, they put hands over shoulders, and put, make a line, and then they start *kicking* them in, kicking them in the back

Similarly, Vasilis (M, 7) explains with concern how the strongest boy in his class picks on one girl whom he dislikes for no apparent reason and beats her up. Jason (M, 7) reports that he has to stop other boys hitting girls in the playground and that, 'some boys go up to girls and get them by their hair, and pull 'em around like that'. One would imagine that boys would not report behaving in such violent ways towards girls themselves but in the case of one particular incident (widely relayed to me in horror by female classmates of the girl concerned), Ryan (M, 8) appeared completely unabashed by his part in this incident and relayed the events with bravado in his interview:

R: See cos erm me an' Sarah had a fight the other day, and I just b- *battered* her up, *mashed* her up, she needed to go and have some *bad injuries* fixed

I: Oh? that's not very nice

R: Not *bad* injuries just some plasters and=

I: Mm (.) what was that about?

R: Oh, she just threw a tennis ball in my face and I went up to 'er, got 'er in a headlock and started beating 'er up

Many of the girls were as large, or larger, than their male counterparts and a few were confident of their physical strength: for example Ketchy (F, 9) and Alma (F, 7) observed that they could beat up any of the boys in their classes. Yet such self-confidence was very rare and most girls appeared intimidated by male physical assertion. Davies (1989, 1993) observed that girls seemed to lack the relevant fantasies required to envisage themselves as physically powerful, whereas the boys were very physical in their interactions as well as having access to fantasies of physical strength (super-heros, sports personalities, etc). Certainly, to judge from their reports, girls in my study appeared almost entirely at the boys' mercy when it came to physical confrontation, although this could have been due to their interview constructions (for instance, they might have been keen to present themselves as victims in order to gain a female adult's sympathy. Similarly, boys might not want to relay incidents of female violence for fear it would undermine their masculine construction of themselves as physically stronger). There was some suggestion in children's reports of boys using violence to censure female behaviour[1]. For example, Veronica (F, 7) relates how one boy, 'says he hates girls (.) but of all the girls he does hate me', and that if she is 'naughty' he violently reprimands her.

It was not only girls who reportedly suffered violence and discrimination at school. Several instances of physical bullying at the hands of other boys were related to me by boys in their interviews. For example, Jason (M, 7) confides that:

J: I'm sometimes *really* naughty, and sometimes I tell mum I don't wanna come to school

I: Why?

J: Cos people hit me

I: Who does?

J: *Big* people (.) children upstairs in other classes

I: Oh no, you should tell Miss Cutter if people are picking on you

J: I have, a few times, but not much happens (.) she, I've told her about Deyo, who's upstairs, and she hasn't done anything about them (.) and there's been loads of complaints about them

I: Have you talked to the headteacher about it?

J: Yes (.) she just has a little conversation about it, and then they don't care, they still do it

I: Do they just bully you do they?

J: Yeh

I: What do you do back?

J: Nothing (.) but now I'm a bit bigger, so my dad tells me to hit back

Whitney and Smith (1993) and Cullingford and Brown (1995) have shown the huge extent of bullying in the primary school, and Whitney and Smith observe that physical bullying is mainly practised by boys against both girls and boys. Grabrucker (1988) has observed that when her young daughter was on the receiving end of violence from boys her age, the response of the boys' parents was that she should 'learn to stand up for herself against boys', as though this would provide gender equality. Grabrucker remarked that the solution should be not for girls to become more violent but for boys to become less so. Bullying is about enforcing power: I suggest that physical bullying due to gender is simply one way of enforcing the gender dichotomy, by both delineating a difference between boys and girls (Skelton, refers to it as boys 'flexing their male power muscles', 1997b, p.359), and policing the maintenance of difference.

Discrimination and sex-stereotyping of activities

Another point occasionally referred to by children reporting incidents of sexism related to boys' gender-differentiation over activities or work. This often involved claims of female inadequacy, or that work is divided into 'men's jobs' and 'women's jobs'. For instance, Roxanne (F, 10) reports how, when water was spilt and the teacher told a boy to clear it up, the boy concerned replied 'That's a *woman's* job'. This type of sexism could apparently be applied to boys as well as girls: earlier, I examined the pressures on boys to take up restrictive masculine constructs. For example, Vanessa (F, 11) relays how, besides girls being told that football is for boys, boys are told that skipping is for girls, and Baresh (M, 8) is told by girls that he cannot play the part of chef in a role-play because men cannot be chefs.

Exclusion from activities

Exclusion of children from activities on account of their gender was frequently alluded to. The example most commonly given was of males refusing to allow girls to play football. This reflects the sex-stereo-typing of activities discussed in Chapter Two: the boys' reported refusal or reluctance to include girls in football games is based on the assumption that girls cannot play football *because* they are girls. In all four schools in my research, the majority of playground space was occupied by boys playing football. Such male domination of the primary school playground has been widely reported[2]. However, the girls in my study claim that besides simply 'hogging' the playground space, many boys were determined to maintain it as exclusively for males. As Vanessa (F, 11) explains, 'Like, if we're playing, if they're playing football, and a girl comes up and says, Can I play, they say No you're a girl, only boys play football'. And Tarlika (F, 11) observes that, 'Like, sometimes when they play football they just say that boys are good at it, girls are – they can't play properly (.) and they sometime don't let, when we just played football today, they just say that I'm not gonna choose you for *my* team'. As Tarlika's words indicate, at each school a few girls were apparently sometimes 'allowed' to participate in the boys' football game.

However, according to many girls and boys there is persistent conflict between genders and anxiety on the part of the girls, as the girls on the periphery of the boys' football space demand to be included in the game. Occasionally the girls reported that individuals or groups of girls were accepted into the game. However, the girls said this was only with explicit permission from the boys, who presented this as a favour and privilege. Moreover, the girls said that once they were allowed into the game, boys often focused on and belittled them. As Sally (F, 11) complains, 'Well, the um, the boys, if they, the girls ask if they can play football, they play, but if they lose they blame it on the girls'. Skelton (1997b) has discussed how playground football gives boys a chance to construct themselves as hegemonically masculine, as the game includes many of these stereotypically masculine aspects (physical strength, speed and stamina; competition, camaraderie and discipline). This may be why many appear so hostile and dismissive of the idea of girls playing football.

In their reports about male exclusion regarding football, girls occasionally complained about some of the very boys who had maintained an egalitarian stance on this issue in their interviews. This discrepancy may have been caused by boys positioning themselves as egalitarian in interaction with a female interviewer while drawing on gender-discriminatory discourse in the playground, or by girls courting the sympathy of a female interviewer by bemoaning the supposed behaviour of specific boys. Short (1993) found that while many children in his study rejected sexist stereotypes during their interviews, they nevertheless participated in gender discriminatory behaviour and concluded that these children, 'lack the courage of their convictions' (p.84). I suggest, however, that rather than children being necessarily hypocritical, they draw on different gender discourses depending on the interactive environment.

Boys were also occasionally reported to be the victims of sexism, by being excluded from certain activities. One class in my study stood out. This Year Six class (10-11 year olds) contained far more girls than boys and this class was peculiar, in that the majority of examples of sexism these children gave involved female discrimination against boys. The single boy in my study who complained that he experienced sexism was in this class: unfortunately I was only able to interview two boys from it, otherwise the figure might have been higher. This situation was reported to stem from a group of girls in the class, headed by Naomi (female, aged 11), who apparently maintained an exclusion policy towards the boys and things male. Thus Sandra's (female, aged 10) example of sexism is that:

S: Well, some girls in my class, they don't um, we have packed lunches boxes and they don't like putting their pack lunch boxes in the same boxes as boys and things, I think it's silly

I: Why is that?

S: I don't know some people just hate boys

She continues,

S: Sometimes the girls won't touch the boys, they, if they touch them accidentally they have to go and wash their hands and things

I: Cos you've got a lot more girls in your class, haven't   [you?

S: [Yeah

I: So do you think it's more in your class, girls being horrible to boys, or is it the other way round as well, or not?

S: (.) Most of the boys are quite friendly, I think it's mostly the girls who are, who're doing that sort of stuff and things

Lucy (F, 10) defines sexism as, 'It's well (.) being, um, (.) when um (.) for example if um a girl hates boys and always goes Ooh I hate boys'. She explains that this happens in her class: 'Well, there's a girl called Naomi, and um like quite a lot of the girls including me um don't like this boy and um, (.) we're always trying to avoid him and if he um, if he comes near us we go Euughh {laughs}'. Naomi (F, 11) herself is the only person who uses her own actions as an example of sexism, when she explains, 'Well like (.) most people have called *me* sexist before because I, I don't exactly go around touching boys and everything (.) and things like that'. When I ask Mark (M, 11) if sexism occurs around the school he replies,

M: *Yeah, Naomi* is cos she doesn't like going next to the boys (.) she moves our bags to the back or something, or=

I: Why d'you think she does that?

M: Cos she doesn't like being next to boys

Mark appears aggrieved by Naomi and her friends' actions, demonstrating that such sexist exclusion by girls can be upsetting. However, despite the high profile of female sexism in this class, Charity (F, 11) observes in her interview that although Naomi is notoriously anti-male (which Charity claims to find stupid), the boys in her class also practice sexist exclusion, refusing to let the girls play football with them.

The children's descriptions of such incidents suggest that forms of sexism may be used by children to aid gender category maintenance. Teasing, exclusion or verbal abuse of the opposite gender may reinforce gender identity by positioning the other gender as 'Other'. Similarly, discrimination and sex-stereotyping remind children of their own gender categories, as well as positioning them as Other through ridicule. Thus all the various manifestations of sexism may be an expression of gender category maintenance used to delineate gender identity, as well as a method of positioning (or being positioned) in relations of power.

How children claim to respond to sexism

All the children who reported to observe sexism in school presented it as unjust. This may have been due to the phraseology of my interview question (the phrase 'picking on' evokes a negative image). This section examines the reports of some of these children about their resistance to sexism. I found six different strategies of resistance in the data: 1) telling a teacher, 2) rebuking the sexist person, 3) ignoring the sexist person, 4) arguing for equality, 5) collective resistance, and 6) demonstration of equality. I now discuss how effective these strategies were, according to the children's reports, in achieving their aims of challenging or avoiding sexism.

Telling a teacher was frequently mentioned as a means of defence or reproof. Lucinda (F, 7) informs me that when boys say girls are weak she retorts, 'if you're going to say that I'm going to tell a teacher', and Catherine (F, 8) tells me that in such instances she would, 'Tell Miss Karner (.) but I wouldn't, beat them up or anything'. This latter answer suggests possible keenness to provide the 'right' answer, which may have motivated more children to say that their response to sexism was to report the incidents to authorities. School ideology maintains that one should inform the teacher when victimised, rather than respond with violence or hostility. However, despite this possible source of exaggeration, complaining to an adult was reported as a resource often utilised by girls in response to the sexism of boys and this suggestion is supported by the findings of Thorne (1993), who maintains that 'telling the teacher' is a strategy commonly used by children of both sexes but most often by girls. Thorne also observes that, though theoretically encouraged in educational environments, 'telling the teacher' often remains frowned-upon by individual teachers as 'telling tales'. She goes on to point out that such attitudes have particularly negative consequences for the girls, as the less physically assertive pupils often have few other forms of recourse. Skelton (1997b) found that girls' complaints about boys' behaviour were often ignored by teachers. The success of this strategy was also thrown into doubt by some children in my study: while Sorrel (F, 10) claims that complaining to a teacher works, the more common response was that telling a teacher worked 'sometimes'.

Two girls described using rebukes to silence sexist boys but said that the boys persist regardless. Kate (F, 10) describes how some of the boys in her class, 'go, Oh women are just, girls are just so *weak*'. Her response is to tell them to be quiet, but she reports that they simply retort, 'You're so weak, you're so weak, you can't tell me what to do'. Similarly Natasha (F, 10) says that one boy in her class, 'always goes that men are better than women'. She tells him that it is not true, yet he persists. Ignoring sexism may be a successful strategy in terms of avoiding sexism or trouble: Salim (M, 10) claims that when he hears people being sexist he 'just moves away from them', as he 'doesn't like getting involved in these things'. While this strategy may save him from becoming involved, it does not challenge sexism in any way. Likewise Vanessa declares that when boys claim that games should be gender-segregated she takes no notice of them as she believes their views to be wrong – but this does not challenge the boys' assumptions.

Other forms of resistance to sexism were reported to be more successful in challenging it. One was argument and dispute of sexism, usually based on theories of gender equality. For instance, Emily (F, 10) says her response to boys' claims to male superiority is to argue, 'we're all equal and we can erm, can all do things, cos we're all good at some things' and Ketchy (F, 9) explains that while she *could* respond to male ridicule of traditionally female roles (such as childcare) with violence, fighting 'isn't allowed in the Bible', so instead she argues that 'feminine' roles like childcare are positive and beneficial. These examples suggest that their competence and familiarity with such egalitarian arguments can have social benefits for girls, by providing a theoretical resource with which to justify their arguments. However, as I argue in Chapter Seven, such equity arguments do not necessarily challenge the fundamental construction of the gender dichotomy.

According to the children's reports, the most effective method of challenging sexism seemed to be by collective resistance: girls (and in some cases, boys too), uniting to confront sexism. Thus Sally (F, 11) describes an instance of successful challenge to a boy's sexist behaviour:

S: (.) Erm, there's *one* person in the class that's mainly sexist to girls

I: Mmm

S: But he *knows* that

I: Right

S: Sometimes girls tell him

I: Yeah, and what does he say about that?

S: Nothing happened

I: No, does he stand up for himself about it though, I mean or- you know, does he carry on, or does he stop because they've said he's sexist?

S: Well, he ain't been doing it as much

I: Hasn't he?

S: No

I: Right (.) why do you think that is?

S: Cos 'e knows he's wrong

I: And is that cos the girls tell him off, or teacher, or what?

S: Erm the girls (.)   [and the boys

I: [the girls, oh that's good then

S: And the boys er, when he gets like that, some of the boys aren't his friend

Thus challenges by girls are given additional support by some boys, with their penalty of withdrawal of friendship, creating an effective strategy against sexism. And Matthew (M, 11) relates another incident of group resistance:

I: And do you ever see anything like that [sexism] happening in class?

M: Yeah, one of the boys in our class always does it

I: Oh right, really? like what?

M: Like, once he said that, men have got real muscles and ladies have got paper muscles

I: {laughs} Oh right, and what did they say?

M: Ehh?

I: What did the girls say to that?

M: They ran after 'im and 'e had to go in the toilets

Such female group resistance has been shown by Lees (1993) to be particularly effective strategy for overcoming male sexism and may have the double benefit of also providing feelings of group solidarity, strength and support amongst the girls and anti-sexist boys.

The final method of resistance to sexism that children reported was one of defiant demonstration by girls that they are equal to boys. Rebecca (F, 8) explains how she proves the boys wrong about female ability at football:

R: I went to play with the boys, but they said No, go away, girls aren't allowed to play football, so I said Why not? They said Girls aren't allowed to be goalies, I said *Why?* (.) and they said Cos girls are prissy-prissy, an' I was wearing high platforms-

I: (.) Mm

R: {sighs} – that day, an' I said, I bet you I could score a goal, with high platforms on, *right* now, from *this* white line, with *all* you stopping me (.) and I did

Sharma (F, 11) describes how boys interrupt constantly and try to dominate conversations, and when I ask if there is a way she deals with such behaviour she replies, 'Mm, yeah (.) I feel like, I say Ohhh, why shouldn't I do it? they do it all the time to me, so I do it to them (.) and inside I think- I, outside I say I'm sorry, but *inside* I'm saying *Yay*, I *done* it'. And when asked how she responds to boys physically picking on girls, Lesley (F, 7) observes, 'Tell teachers, but sometimes we *don't* (.) cos we can (.) really, boys that are older think they can *attention* us, just cos we're *younger*, but I take no notice of them (.) I don't take much notice of them, if 'e bullied *me* I'd bully 'im back, I don't care what Miss'd say, I'd just stand firm'. Thus these children describe themselves assertively supporting their claims to equality with demonstrations of their equal ability.

The strategies described as most effective in challenging sexism appeared to be those supported either by equity arguments or by demonstration of equal capability. However, such strategies required assertive challenges, and some girls may be too intimidated by sexism to attempt such methods. Moreover, such behaviour may not fit the girls' construction of female identity as passive or facilitating as opposed to masculine constructions[3]. These findings regarding children's descriptions of resistance to sexism in school *suggest* that some sexism may be contested by children. As the data here simply draws on children's interview reports, a further, observational study of children's interaction in the primary school would be required to examine these suggestions more fully.

Discussion

To recap, about 80% of girls and 60% of boys claimed that they had observed sexism in the primary school. Nearly two-thirds of the girls claimed to have experienced sexism at the hands of the boys in school. So according to the pupils, gender is commonly a source of discrimination, and this discrimination is mainly practised against girls (although we noted some instances of female sexism). Analysing the children's reports it appears that their constructions of the genders as polarised may have real social consequences, resulting in sexism and discrimination. Not all children constructed gender as a source of discrimination in school, however: a minority, mainly boys, did not report observing sexism in the primary school. Because of the nature of this study (reliance on interview reports rather than classroom observation) it is impossible to know whether the children's reports accurately reflected classroom experience. However, it is important to note how many children constructed sexism as occurring in the classroom and impacting on their lives. This finding, supported by observational research such as Skelton's, is a cause for teacher concern. Skelton (1997b) found that teachers tended to ignore incidents where primary school boys sexually intimidated girls, dismissing it as 'routine naughtiness' (p.353). As a consequence girls understand the message that this problem is not seen as important, and Skelton observes that after a period of time girls had given up reporting such incidents. This has important implications: not only do girls end up suffering in silence, but they also read the message that such male behaviour is normal, even acceptable. That so many children construct sexism as impacting on their lives at school demonstrates that teachers must take complaints about sexism, whether verbal or physical, seriously.

As well as enforcing power relationships, sexism may be an excess of the gender category maintenance processes used by children to demonstrate their gender identity. Many different methods of resistance to sexism were described by children, and some were reported as more succesful than others: according to the children's descriptions, the most effective were those that required assertion and confrontation. However, it is possible that traits such as these may be undeveloped by girls in mixed sex interaction, as they conflict with the dominant construction of femininity. Once again we return to the root problem of the construction of the gender dichotomy, where the construction of genders as different must be maintained by conformity to gendered behaviour and enforced by gender category maintenance. Chapter Eight considers ways in which the gender dichotomy itself might be challenged.

Notes

1)   see also Herbert (1989), and Lees (1993), for descriptions of the way in which school boys use violence and sexual harassment to regulate girls' behaviour.

2)   Whyte (1986), Davies (1989), and Thorne (1993) all report how boys dominate the playground in terms of the amount of space they take up.

3)   See Walkerdine (1990) for an explanation of the gender dichotomy; and Francis (1998), as well as Chapter Five of this book, for a developed description of the ways in which children construct the genders as oppositional by taking up opposite types of behaviour.

CHAPTER 5

THE CONSTRUCTION OF OPPOSITIONAL GENDER CULTURES IN THE ROLE-PLAYS

This chapter is about the children's role-plays about adult work. Children's choice and acting of work roles in the plays are investigated to see whether they are gender-stereotypical. The issue of their oppositional gender constructions is also revisited, showing how these oppositional positions resulted in the formation of symbolic gender cultures amongst children during their interaction.

Who got first choice?

In the mixed sex role-plays it was most often boys or one boy in particular who chose the role-play scenario: out of 15 mixed sex groups, boys chose the scenario in 11. Boys also gained first choice of role in 11.5 of these 15 plays (in one group a boy and a girl chose the same job at the same time and both refused to accept any other, which accounts for the 0.5). The most powerful role was not always chosen first; the taking up of powerful roles is discussed in the next chapter. During the choice of scenario and role, girls were sometimes unassertive, simply accepting the last role or even explicitly leaving the choice up to the boys (again, this is discussed more fully in Chapter Six). Yet more often the boys got their way simply by adamantly insisting on their choice – for instance repeating it over and over again – rather than compromising or reaching a group agreement. Although this tactic was occasionally used by girls, the boys employed it far more frequently. It led to some problems in the boys-only role-play groups – in the mixed groups girls would often accommodate the boys' demands, whereas in the boys-only groups a situation occasionally developed where two or more boys were equally determined to have the same role and doggedly refused to compromise.

Table 1 shows the number of times each scenario was chosen. The hospital scenario was chosen only by Year Three groups, whereas ten out of fifteen Year Six groups chose the hotel scenario.

Table 1: Choices of role play scenario in all role play groups

SCENARIO:	SCHOOL	HOTEL	HOSPITAL
Year Three children	6	6	4
Year Four children	0	1	0
Year Five children	2	0	0
Year Six children	5	10	0
Total	13	17	4

Table 2 shows the numbers of girls and boys who chose the various roles in the mixed sex groups, allowing us to see whether or not girls and boys took up gender-stereotypical roles in the plays. Some of the occupational roles are difficult to stereotype: for instance, the broad term 'room service attendant' could have been understood as a traditionally male bell-hop or a traditionally female maid, or simply not recognised by children at all and so not stereotyped. Others may have been interpreted in different ways by children: for example, although 'chef' is a traditionally male role, this did not always seem to have been understood, particularly by the younger children. Many girls took on the role and called themselves 'cook' and there was one incident when a boy was told by girls in his group that chef is a women's job.

Children took up gender-stereotypical roles when playing 'hospital' on both occasions, with boys playing doctor and girls playing nurse and receptionist. I suggest that 'patient' was only played by boys because

Table 2: Mixed sex group's choice of roles:

ROLE	Played by Girl	Played by Boy
Hospital		
Doctor	0	2
Hospital Receptionist	2	0
Nurse	2	0
Patient	0	2
Hotel		
Chef	4	5
Hotel Receptionist	7	3
Manager	4	5
Room Service Attendant	4	4
School		
Caretaker	0	4
Head teacher	2	2
Playground Supervisor	3	1
Teacher	3	1
TOTAL:	31	29

(in one group there were three girls and one boy).

of the gender-stereotyped nature of the other roles in the hospital scenario: if doctor is chosen by a boy, and nurse and receptionist by the girls, only the role of patient is left for the second boy. The choice of roles and the gender dichotomies they present (for instance, doctor/ nurse), may have had an impact on children's choices due to the gender dynamic in the mixed groups. The 'school' scenario offered one stereo- typically male role (caretaker), while the others are stereotypically female (playground supervisor and teacher), or neutral (headteacher).

So gender-casting was not so easy, leading to more variety in children's choices. Choices of role in the hotel scenario showed by far the most variety according to gender. As noted above, gender-typing the roles in this scenario may have been problematic. However, the majority of children conducting plays with this scenario were from the older age-groups, most of whom were familiar with the occupational roles involved. Thus of all three scenarios, 'hotel' involved occupational roles which the children gender-stereotyped the least often.

Children's contrasting constructions of gender and occupation in the role-plays and interviews

In their role-plays children tended to construct gender differently from the way they did in their interviews: their constructions change depending on the interactive environment. According to Billig (1987), for each argument we make we necessarily have some idea of a counter-argument. We use different arguments depending on our respondent. Thus, Billig argues, attitudes and arguments should be placed in their 'rhetorical context'. Similarly, Shotter (1989) observes that an addresser always considers what the receiver's response might be: as one is attempting to 'mean' something to someone else, an assessment of how they might respond is part of our construction of who they are for us. So we draw upon different arguments depending on our respondent or, in post-structuralist terms, different discourses depending on the discursive environment. Buckingham (1993) provides an example in his study which supports this argument, suggesting that black children in an inner city school were much keener to draw attention to their racial identity than those in a suburban school. In the suburban school the black children comprised a fragile minority group, so tried to discursively position themselves as similar to the white children, rather than risk calling attention to their difference. My research similarly found that children's constructions of gender and adult occupation were sometimes different in role-play groups than in their individual responses to a female adult interviewer.

Various factors may have contributed to such differences. The drama background of the role-play groups allowed children to adopt different positions and constructions to those which they took up in the interviews: they are *acting* in the role-plays and therefore had the opportunity to present constructions which they might normally reject. That children take up different constructions shows that they are aware of, and can draw on, a variety of gender discourses. Chapter Seven discusses where such different ideas about gender might come from.

Many children constructed the genders more stereotypically in the role-plays than in the individual interviews. For instance, Simon (M, 11), playing hotel manager, made an allegation of sexual misconduct against a girl in the play in order to humiliate her (this incident is discussed further in Chapter Six). He used his high-status position of manager to exercise power by drawing attention to Sabina's (F, 10) low-status position and femininity. Yet during his individual interview Simon argued for equal opportunities, positioning himself as egalitarian. Likewise, while Peter (M, 8) shunned the role of nurse in a hospital role-play, he said in his following interview that if the boy who accepted the role had played another part, he (Peter) would have willingly played nurse. Other stereotypes of adult work appeared in role-plays but not in interviews: in an all-female role-play (Year Three girls), Jade (F, 8), who is playing room service attendant, repeatedly addressed the girl playing the hotel manager as 'Sir', demonstrating her construction of manager as a male role. In her interview, however, Jade said that women and men can do the same jobs, and supported equal opportunities. Some children seemed to assume that 'two roles are for girls, two roles are for boys' in the mixed sex role-play groups: during the role choice of a hospital play, Angela (F, 10) volunteered, 'I'll be, the nurse (.) or receptionist or whatever', although in her interview discussion she maintained that women can do the same jobs as men.

Other children drew upon gender-discriminatory ideas more in the interviews than the role-plays. In some role-plays gender was not alluded to verbally at all, whereas in the interviews many of the questions were specifically concerned with gender. Thus the interviews elicited comments on gender in a way that the role-plays did not, and consequently many children articulated gender-discriminatory ideas which did not appear in the role-plays (see previous chapters). On one occasion, however, Chantelle (F, 11) appears in her interview about the play to construct genders as more different from each other than she did in the play itself:

I: Right, you chose the manager didn't you, why was that?

C: (.) He'd be leader

I: (.) Right (.) and you think it'd be a 'he'?

C: (.) Nah, or a 'she'

She felt able to position herself as manager in the play but constructed the role as male in her talk with me.

Thus children drew upon gender-discriminatory discourses in some social contexts and equity discourses in others. These apparently contrary positions examplify the multiple and often contradictory discursive positions available to us in different interactive environments. Moreover, children were *acting* in the role-plays: they could draw on different constructions because of the plays' fantasy quality. Of Simon's accusation about Sabina's (F, 10) sexual misconduct, Nima (M, 10) observes that although Simon should not have made the claim, he probably felt it was acceptable because they were doing a play and, 'when you're acting you can say all sorts of things'. Ironically, Nima goes on to say that although Sabina probably felt angry and 'wanted to slap' Simon, she could not because, 'they were acting so she had to put up with it'. This suggests that while the play environment lessened Simon's inhibitions, allowing him to make a sexist accusation against Sabina, Sabina's subordinate role in the play restricted and inhibited her, reducing her ability to retaliate.

However, children generally appeared to gender-stereotype adult occupations more in the plays than in their interview talk. Nima's comment, that you can 'say all sorts of things' in plays, suggests an explanation for this: children may have drawn on a wider variety of gender constructions in their acting than in their talk with me. For example, there was some evidence of children drawing on media ideas and evidence in the role-play data: Baresh (M, 8) supports his claim to the role of chef by noting that he has seen male chefs in films, and Cally (F, 10) appears to draw on melodramatic screen narratives as manager in her hotel play, declaring to her usurpers, 'How dare you? the hotel is my *life*... I will *not* leave, I demand it!... By a woman's right to decide it, I will *not leave!*'. It is also possible, however, that in their interaction with other children (rather than just with an adult female interviewer), the children construct the genders as more polarised.

The constructions of children in 'non-gender-appropriate' roles

This section examines the taking up of the role 'nurse' in a male role-play group, and the role of 'caretaker' in a female group. Only one all-male group chose the hospital scenario, and I was interested to see how the 'doctors and nurses' dichotomy was handled by the boys. This was the *only* instance where a boy had to play nurse: as we saw above, in both mixed hospital role-plays a girl took up the role. In the all-male group no-one wanted to play nurse and there was much giggling and embarrassment about this, although the boys never explicitly verbalised the reason for their unwillingness. This may have been because of my presence as a female adult. As all the other roles had been taken Denzel (M, 7) was left with the role but he did not want it. At this point Johnnie (M, 7) noted tentatively that men can be nurses too and I supported this point by remarking that the television pro-gramme *Casualty* portrays male as well as female nurses. There was general hesitant agreement and at this point Ryan (M, 8) generously volunteered to play nurse. I use the word 'generously' without irony, as this is how his gesture appeared to be interpreted by the rest of the group: he had been the martyr and thus saved them from having to play the gender-stigmatised role. In fact Ryan was spared from any derision or ridicule for playing the role. This may have been because his generosity earned him the gratitude and respect of the rest of the group or possibly because of his social position in the group (he may have been popular). This illustrates the complex, fluctuating and multiple nature of power positionings in interaction.

The reaction of this group to the role of 'nurse' suggests that they con-structed the role as stereotypically feminine and thus stigmatised, and consequently feared to be associated with such a role in front of the other males in the group. As Buckingham (1993) observes of boys' group interaction, boys' sense of their masculinity appears very fragile in their discussions but seems extremely important to them and depends on mutual support and policing. Other research has presented a similar picture of fragile, mutually constructed masculinity[1]. The interaction described above appears to depict an incident of collective support against a potentially humiliating challenge to masculinity.

Another role which was taken up as particularly gendered was care-taker. This was almost universally accepted as a male role: in mixed sex groups it was always taken up by boys and even in the female role-plays the acceptance of the role was usually reluctant, leaving the player open to ridicule from the other girls. The girls in single-sex groups who took up (or were left with) this role nearly always attempted to turn the role and their acceptance of it into a joke, the more self-confident girls acting in a comically exaggerated masculine manner and referring to themselves as 'Mr So-and-so'. The school scenario may well have been influenced by the real-life staff that children saw around them at their own schools every day. All the schools had women headteachers, and a relatively high number of girls took up this role: the girls may have seen this as evidence that the role was open to them. In the same way, all the schools had male caretakers and it may be no coincidence that this was the school role children retained as exclusively male. In a Year Three girls groups at St. Luke's school, everyone has chosen roles apart from Emmi (F, 7); caretaker is all that's left:

K: {murmurs to Emmi who smiles, cringes, and covers mouth with hands. Kelly turns to look at me with anticipation}

C: {smiling, to me} What's *she* {Emmi} gonna have to be?

I: Mm?

C: What's she gonna have to be?

I: The caretaker's the other one (.) {the three girls with parts burst into loud giggles, and Emmi pulls a 'gobsmacked' face} Why's that funny?

K: I dunno

C: Dunno

S: No (.) go on Emmi {they are all still grinning. Emmi is playing with a card}

C: Go on, you've *got* to, it's all that's left {all looking at Emmi who fiddles with card}

K: Caretaker would be good, {gestures brightly} like, polishing and everything

C: *Yeah*

K: And er=

E: {sighing and raising eyes to heavens} *Okay*

K: =telling people to get out of my floor, and things like that

I: 'Kay, can you say what you all are?

S: {to me} Playground supervisor

C: {to me} Teacher

E: (.) {looks at me, smiles} Caretaker {looks into her lap. Kelly giggles again}

I: Caretaker, okay {Kelly goes on sniggering and looking at Emmi}

Clearly the masculine role of caretaker is depicted as ridiculous in this all-female group, suggesting the girls constructed the role as Other and inferior. Possibly the girls could also have been put off by the perceived menial, manual nature of a caretaker's work but this arguably also holds gendered connotations. Moreover, in this case Emmi is finally persuaded (reluctantly) to take up the role of caretaker when Kelly embellishes it with feminine qualities ('polishing and everything'). This does not prevent Kelly from continuing to laugh at Emmi's role, suggesting that Kelly's presentation of caretaker in a more positive light is simply a ploy to persuade Emmi to take up the role, while simultaneously presenting herself in the sensible, conciliatory, almost motherly mode so favoured by girls. When, in her interview, I asked Sonia (F, 7) why they were laughing at Emmi in the play, she replied, 'Well, cos caretakers are normally *men*, and Emmi's a wo- er, Emmi's a *girl* {laughs}'. Being left with the role constructed as masculine and being pressured to take it up by her sneering contemporaries, appears painful to Emmi. She tries to make the best of it by portraying her humorous dislike of her position to distance herself from it in front of the other girls (rolling her eyes, groaning, etc.), but her anxiety and embarrassment are evident from her fidgeting with the card and her lowered eyes. Association with things masculine and menial appeared to be as humiliating in this all-female group as was association with things feminine in the all-male group.

Processes of gender category maintenance are evident in both these groups. Taking up a non-gender-appropriate role is in both cases presented as a cause for anxiety and potential ridicule. Where the boys collectively and supportively uphold their masculinity, the girls *not* playing caretaker seem to bond in femininity in their ridicule of Emmi's masculine position.

Children's construction of gender cultures in the role-plays

The preference for taking up roles which are associated with the child's own gender may be part of the wider pattern of gender category maintenance. The extent to which they presented gender as oppositional in their discussions with me (see Chapter Two), was matched in their role-play interaction with one another. This had the effect of constructing gender cultures which were opposite and in opposition in the role-play groups. The different ways in which these symbolic cultures were constructed and maintained in children's role-play interaction are now discussed.

Portraying genders as in opposition

In the previous chapter it was argued that forms of sexism are used by children for gender category maintenance, in that they help to delineate gender identity. Reactionary comments about gender were sometimes used by children, particularly boys, during mixed sex group interaction, to define the opposition of the genders clearly. A reactionary comment might provoke an outraged or hurt reaction from the targeted party, consequently positioning the speaker as clearly separate from the other gender and thus bonded with their own gender group. We see this during a Year Six mixed sex role-play when Carlie asks the chef (Nima) how he cooks at home and he replies with a grin, 'My wife does the cooking, innit?', provoking an outraged gasp from Sabina who reacts, 'I think the woman *and* man should cook'. Through such means boys can highlight their maleness before the rest of the group, aiding male bonding. Reactionary comments can be used to evoke gender differences, so strengthening gender identities and helping to construct the separate gender cultures.

This sort of behaviour could be seen in the role-play groups. Many of the girls portrayed boys as completely different and even inferior to themselves. This was particularly common and strongly worded in the all-female role-play groups: girls frequently derided boys for showing

off and being silly or rough. When they find they have too much work
to do in their female-only group, Sharma (F, 11) suggests they recruit
some boys. Sandra (F, 10) reacts by yelling an emphatic '*No way!*' and
is supported by nods from the other girls. This female bonding is
illustrated by another all-girl group (a Year Three group at St. Luke's),
who construct a collective fantasy of power over 'the boys' during their
role-play. They are playing a school scenario in which they try to tackle
the litter problem:

I: So tell me your plan all together then, you're gonna warn them in
     assembly=

K: And like, if they don't, do as they're told, we can like ban the people from
     their playtime, ban, [if it's boys, ban them from basketball, make them write
     poetry=

E: [Yeah, from the school

K: =write poetry, cos our class absolutely *hates* poetry

C: (.) And there'll   [be, no playtime

S: [Yeah and (.) {to Charis}   [no=

E: [Or if it was boys I'd,
     I'd kill them {laughs}

K: We'd ban football

I: Right

K: [From them=

S: [And they um, could get detention

C: Yeah

E: [Or we could get=

I: [How would you tell if it was boys or girls?

C: [Well

K: [Umm

S: Cos boys are more [naughtier

K: [Boys are mischievous

C: {leaning forward} Yeh boys are more, like, naughtier, y'know?

E: Or we could even ban them from basketball

K: Or foot [ball

C: [And football

K: Cos they're normally playing basketball=

S: No, football

K: Or give them detention

C: And, yeah, ban them from their playtime

The attitude of 'them and us' can be strongly felt in this extract, as well as the mutual enjoyment in envisaging ways to make the boys suffer. Thus children's presentations of the genders as in opposition in these instances aided in-gender bonding and constructed separate gender cultures.

Portraying the genders as opposite: the construction of a sensible selfless/silly selfish dichotomy in children's interaction

The construction of gender as opposite leads children to take up gendered types of behaviour in role-play, which reflected the dichotomous 'sensible selfless' (feminine) and 'silly selfish' (masculine) constructions noted in the second chapter. This construction of female as sensible and selfless and male as silly and selfish forms the basis of the two gender cultures in the primary school. Of the feminine construction, maturity, obedience and neatness are the 'sensible' qualities. These lead to 'selflessness' – giving, facilitating, compromising and placing others first (martyrdom) – in an attempt to appear mature and sensible. The masculine construction involves 'silly' qualities of immaturity, messiness and naughtiness, leading to 'selfishness' – taking, demanding and refusing to compromise. Obviously the majority of children do not take up these gendered qualities all the time or in any consistent way, but the two cultures are constructed as opposite, by means of the exaggeration of feminine and masculine behaviour by children through their gender category maintenance. Thus masculine behaviour comes to be reviled by many girls, who contruct their feminine culture as superior to that of the boys, and vice versa.

This point is illustrated by the scorn of things male on the part of individual girls, and particularly all-girl groups. The assertions by Sonia (F, 7), Kelly (F, 8) and Charis (F, 7) that boys are 'naughtier' and 'more mischievous' than girls are typical of girls' statements about boys. There were many instances where girls positioned themselves as sensible and/ or selfless in contrast to the boys' constructions in the mixed sex group interaction. Shamim (F, 7) tells me that girls are 'more sensible than boys'. Likewise when Junior (M, 10) cheekily asks if we have finished the role-play yet, Karen (F, 10) says 'no' in shocked outrage and reprimands Junior by pretending to whack him with the back of her hand. And when I ask a Year Three mixed sex group whether they have found a solution to the role-play problem, Maddie (F, 7) looks at Cathleen (F, 7) for support and declares, 'I think we should try better'.

Selfless positions were also much in evidence among the girls in mixed sex groups: when I ask which role-play scenario a Year Three mixed sex group would like, Angela (F, 7) volunteers, 'I don't really mind' and in another, Lucy (F, 10) replies, 'Let the boys decide'. Karen (F, 10) originally says she wants the role of manager as I list the role choices but immediately turns to the two boys in her group and asks, 'can I be manager?' and then allows a boy to choose manager instead. And when in her interview I congratulate Emily (F, 10) on her creative ideas in the role-play, she modestly replies, 'Well I don't really think so but I thought, I thought Nancy's ideas were very good'. Many girls presented boys as sillier, naughtier and ruder than girls, indicating not just a feeling of difference from boys but also a feeling of disapproval and distaste at their masculine culture. However, their sensible-selfless positions had ramifications on girls' power positions in the mixed sex interaction, as I discuss in the next chapter.

These sensible-selfless positions were by no means consistent, as the above discussion of the Year Three girls' 'school' role-play demonstrates: the three girls *not* playing the role of caretaker hardly evoke 'sensible-selflessness' as they sneer at their fellow. Yet throughout the role-play the four girls refer to 'the boys' with disapproval and position themselves as sensible compared to the children they describe as badly behaved and whom Charis (F, 7) brands 'those sorts of people'. So this particular group of girls apparently constructed themselves as sensible, despite their sometimes contrary behaviour. Similarly, the boys did not always take up the opposite silly, selfish position – as we saw in the role-plays discussed earlier. In the Year Three boys' hospital role-play, Ryan (M, 8) selflessly takes up the unwanted role of nurse and the other boys' response is tactful, not silly.

Yet there was much other evidence that boys constructed a male gender-cultural position of 'silly selfishness' in opposition to the female gender-cultural position of 'sensible selflessness'. For instance, in a Year Three mixed sex role-play, the boys' behaviour becomes sillier and more immature the more the girls self-righteously complain about it. It was noticeable that the boys were not in the least abashed by the reproaches and scorn of their female counterparts. Rather, they appeared to expect and relish the female disapproval, suggesting that these two positions have become ritualised in children's mixed sex interaction[2]. This also applies to boys' 'silly' talk about violence: like Buckingham (1993), Jordan (1995) and Vicks (1990), I found that boys often allude to or fantasise about violence, particularly in mixed sex groups. For example, in a Year Three mixed sex group acting a school scenario, Noel (M, 7) plays headteacher. His contributions focus on possible punishments or deterrents for children dropping litter:

'And when they're putting rubbish in the bin, I can hide in the bin, and I can jump out and go {leans towards mike} *Boo*'

'=And then the children come over here, and I *shout* at them'

'And I can smash 'em [children] up', 'Yeah, ooh, and then I could, do karate on them'

'Yeah and then we could smash = {speaking louder to be heard} we could smash their heads through the windows'.

As Buckingham (1993) argues, talking about violence (or emotions), or refusing to, should be perceived as a social act rather than an indication of a violent 'nature'. Boys' 'liking for violence' can be seen as another 'masculine' sign used by boys to construct their masculinity. This interpretation is supported by Jordan's (1995) finding that boys construct themselves as masculine by positioning themselves as 'Other' to girls (and 'wimpy' boys) through violent fantasy play.

These dichotomous 'sensible selfless/silly selfish' constructions of gender also explain why a greater number of boys gained first choice of role-play scenario and role than did the girls. The 'silly selfish' positions allowed boys to take their first choices of role (often the most powerful ones) in the plays, by assertively jumping in first, or demanding the role so confidently, loudly and persistently, that others gave in. Once they had 'bagged' a role, most boys adamantly insisted on keeping it. The 'sensible selfless' feminine construction complimented this, with many girls giving up their chosen role to a boy or simply accepting the remaining role which no-one else wanted.

By positioning the genders as relational and oppositional, children construct two symbolic gender cultures. This was achieved in the role-plays by presenting the genders as in opposition and as opposite. However, just as such oppositional constructions did not occur all the time or in any rigid way, not all the children appeared to perceive two clearly delineated gender cultures. And not all the children who did see two separate cultures were happy with the constructions or supported gender category maintenance. Resistance and contradiction to the constructed gender cultures is discussed next.

Resistance and contradiction to the gender boundaries

Despite the opposition of the two gender cultures and the rigorous gender category maintenance processes enforcing these gender boundaries, much border-crossing *did* take place, as Thorne (1993) observed in her study of children's construction of gender roles in primary schools. Some girls and boys took up non-gender-stereotypical roles: Baresh (M, 8) even argues with the girls in his group who claim that he should not play the role he wants because 'men can't cook'. Likewise, as we saw above, by no means all children adhered to the dichotomy in which the female is sensible and selfless and the male silly and selfish. These gendered constructions were taken up by some children at certain times and often contained contradictions.

It must also be remembered that gender constructions exist alongside a multitude of other power factors which can combine with or outweigh these. During the Year Three girl's group role-play where caretaker is positioned as Other, we find that not all girls automatically win approval simply by being female. When I ask the group whether its fantasy of punishing the boys is a fair one, Kelly points out that girls could be dropping litter as well:

K: Cos like, some people like, some girls and boys act, like um,[like um act cool and like, do naughty things

C: [Yeah (.)

    [Yeah

S: [Like   Sophina

K: Yeah, [Sophina

C: [Sophina

K: She, she like plays with=

S: And Tyrone and Stallone, and   [Leke

K: [Leke

Here a school-orientated, 'sensible selfless' construction positions *naughtiness* as outweighing the gender-cultural construction of female gender unity in opposition to things masculine which previously motivated the group. The girls in the group self-righteously position themselves as separate from 'naughty' boys *and* girls. (We can also see the disapproval Sophina receives from this female group for crossing gender-boundaries, another form of gender category maintenance). Many other factors may also impact upon children's constructions: race, social class, and whether a child is popular, are but a few (see Thorne, 1993, Davies, 1993). So gender was constructed as opposite by children in some circumstances and not in others.

Summary

To conclude, the taking up of roles in the plays did appear gendered: although many children did *not* take up gender-stereotypical roles in the mixed sex groups, the majority did. I suggest that the choice of gender-traditional roles in the plays is due to gender category maintenance on the part of children, who take up gender as integral to their social identity, and who rely on symbolic demonstration to prove their gender. Children's constructions of gender in the role-plays about adult work often differed from their interview constructions. Their presentation of gender and occupation was often more stereotypical in the role-plays, suggesting that in their acting children drew on a wider, or different, range of ideas about gender. They may also be keener to adopt gender stereotypical constructions when interacting with their peers, due to the pressures of gender category maintenance. Turning to their own gender constructions in the plays, I suggest that gendered differences in behaviour are due to the symbolic gender cultures. These dichotomous cultures are constructed in children's interaction via gender category maintenance and, consequently, identification with a particular construction of gender. The cultures are constructed through in-gender bonding where children position the genders as opposite and in opposition in order to reinforce their own sense of gender identity. However, these cultures are not fixed, being simply the manifestation of children's different constructions. Gender boundaries were frequently crossed and gender was only one aspect of children's social constructions.

Notes

1) See, for example, the work on constructions of masculinity by Middleton (1992), Mac an Ghaill (1994), Hearn and Morgan (1995), Jordan (1995), Connell (1995), Skelton (1997b) and Tett (1997).

2) Thorne (1993) observes that where gender boundaries are evoked they are often accompanied by stylised, ritualised forms of action, and like Davies (1989) she observed the way children use this ritualised behaviour to denote gender identity. This ritual action sometimes involved the construction of the genders as rival groups and thus *in opposition* in school. However, she notes children can and frequently do cross and resist gender boundaries.

CHAPTER 6

CHILDREN'S CONSTRUCTIONS OF GENDER AND POWER IN THE ROLE-PLAYS

This chapter examines children's constructions of gender as a source of power in their role-play interaction. It investigates the actual impact made by children's constructions of gender on their positions of power.

As was observed in the first chapter, post-structuralist approaches have been criticised by writers such as Soper (1990, 1993a), Davis (1988) and Lloyd and Duveen (1992) for failing to address the way that certain social groups can exercise power over others. I am using the word 'power' as Foucault (1980) did, to describe the fluid positionings of selves through discourse. However, I am also seeking to examine the social outcomes of these positionings in terms of gender. In other words, I want to look at the production of reality through gender discourse and its consequences for children's interaction. In his work exploring nature discourses, Macnaghten (1993) attempts to relate the constructions of nature to the realities they produce – to examine the connection between the constructions and their 'material outcome' (p.56). Following Macnaghten, I seek to explore the outcome of children's use of gender discourses, aiming to link discourses to the realities they produce.

Several researchers have discussed how children position themselves and are positioned in discourse. Buckingham (1993) and Middleton (1992) mainly discuss this issue concerning children's positioning of *themselves* in certain ways during social interaction: Buckingham

(1993) shows how children used talk about television to position themselves powerfully in interaction. Examining how children are *positioned* in discourse, Walkerdine (1988, 1989, 1990, 1997), Jordan (1995) and Davies (1989) catalogue the ways in which girls are produced as inadequate through dominant, male-centred gender discourses. Davies' (1989) argument that the dominant discursive practice which positions all people as male or female also positions power as *male* power was noted in Chapter One. She argues that female power is legitimate only in the domestic realm or as helpers of boys and men. This chapter investigates whether girls took up powerful positions in the role-play groups and how children were positioned through gender discourses during their interaction.

The power positions created for subjects are often multiple and contradictory[1]. Moreover, as we saw in the previous chapter, gender discourses are by no means the only ones drawn on by children in the production of power positions: they exist and compete alongside a myriad of other discourses, which can sometimes outweigh those of gender. I have reported instances of this in other chapters: for example, Chapter Three showed how a large proportion of children, particularly girls, implied that the power of a woman boss derived from her occupational status would outweigh the power derived from gender of her male subordinates. However, for the purposes of this investigation I intend to focus mainly on power positioning regarding *gender* discourse.

I begin by analysing the ways in which children were positioned by others, and positioned themselves and others during the role-plays. This issue is examined in the contexts of both the single and the mixed sex, groups. I return to the issue of the sensible selfless/silly selfish constructions discussed in the last chapter, maintaining that these constructions lead many girls and boys to position themselves in particular ways within the plays. It is argued that in the mixed sex groups the boys' higher status roles, gained because of the girls' sensible-selfless constructions, can be combined with gender discourse to position the other group members as subordinate, and thus to dominate the play. Instances were also found when children did not appear to construct gender as a source of power in the role-plays, and this point is discussed. But children's gendered constructions generally impacted upon their power positions in the role-plays.

Constructions of power in single-sex groups

I wanted to see what forms children's constructions of gender and power took in single-sex groups, and whether these differed between the boys' and girls' groups.

The sensible selfless/silly selfish dichotomy in the single-sex groups

There was some evidence that the 'sensible selfless' positions (which I reported many girls using in their construction of oppositional gender cultures) could be used powerfully by girls in single-sex role-play groups. An example is the case of Nancy and Charity. To make up the numbers, Nancy (F, 11) and Charity (F, 11) took part in two girls' group role-plays. This meant that in the second play they had knowledge of the role-play process not shared by the other girls – so took up positions as facilitating quasi-teachers. Teacher-like, they explained the role-play process and asked the other girls which roles they would like, thus appearing sensible and selfless. Yet due to the respect these positions elicited from the other girls, Nancy and Charity used their mediative position to manipulate the other two girls and the course of the play: they chose the role-play scenario and directed events. So in a female single-sex role-play this sensible selfless position appeared a powerful one, which the girls could use to their advantage in terms of power position.

The boys' positions of silly selfishness became difficult to maintain in single-sex boys' groups. In the previous chapter I described how girls facilitated boys' demands in many mixed sex groups, allowing the boys first choice of scenario or role, or resignedly accepting the last role (this issue is explored more fully later in this chapter). In the all-boy groups the lack of compromise in boys' silly selfish positions lead to occasional problems: there were more arguments over choice of role in the boys' plays than the girls' single-sex plays. The following transcript extract is a rather extreme example of a struggle over roles in a Year Three boys' role-play. First there was domination rather than co-operation in the group's choice of scenario:

I: Hotel is one of the choices, or you could choose school, or you could choose hospital

C: Hospital   [hospital

M: [Hospital

K: [Hotel, hotel   [hotel

S: [Hotel

M: Hotel

C: *Hospital*

M: Three against one

K: Yeh, hotel, yeh yeh [hotel, hotel

S: [Hotel, hotel, I wanna be the=

C: Okay, hotel

Then there was further conflict over the choice of roles, as Kalpesh (M, 7), Chris (M, 7) and Mike (M, 7) reached deadlock over who will take the role of manager:

K: Manager,   [manager

M: Manager

I: It's not up to me

C: Manager

M: [Manager, manager {Kalpesh and Mike both have their hands up and get up from their seats to stand while chanting}

K: [Manager, manager

M: {pulling fist back at Kalpesh} I'm the manager

K: {raising fist} I'm manager, manager , [manager

M: {waving fist threateningly}   [*I'm* manager, you
     wanna=?

I: *Shhhh,* and   [keep sitting down=

M: {to Kalpesh} [Don't make me, I'm   [manager

K: [*I'm man-e-ger* {he sits, and
     Mike follows suit

M: Manager

Chris eventually decided to be chef, but Kalpesh and Mike continued in the same vein, despite the increasing impatience of the other two boys:

M: {to Kalpesh} Be receptionist, cos you can tell anyone to get out now=

K: {turns his back and folds his arms} No I ain't gonna be that, [I wanna be the manager

M: [I'm the

manager, I'm the manager

K: *Manager*

M: I'm the manager

C: {gestures in annoyance} Oh,   [just get *started*

K: [Manager manager, I'm the   [manager

and that's final

M: [I'm the

manager, I'm the manager

K: [I'm the manager, and that's final

S: [..... {says something to me}

M: *I'm* manager, and that's, *fullstop*

S: (.) {to Kalpesh} Yeah, what will you [be?

K: {whipping around}   [I'm manager, an' thass *final*

M: {gestures for emphasis} Double full stop, full full stop, thass *final* (.) no, *I'm* final that *I'm* the manager {noise off camera} (.) who's doing that, a ghost?

C: {laughs} Hurry up

M: I'm the manager man, look, I said it last, I'm manager I'm manager I'm manager, I'm manager I'm manager I'm manager

S: Duhhh {sighs}

Eventually I had to suggest that we toss a coin for the role, as they refused to reach agreement co-operatively. In this case it could be argued that the boys' silly, selfish constructions actually disadvantaged them, as it prevented them and the other group members from progressing with the play and they earned my disapproval. However, perhaps they did not *want* to progress with the play, or my approval (in fact, as Skelton's (1997) work illustrates, 'getting one over the teacher' can play a part in boys' construction of hegemonic masculinity. Although not an official teacher I was still perceived by the children as an adult authority figure).

The use of comedy and violent talk to gain status in single-sex groups

In the single-sex role-plays girls often used humour to make the other girls laugh, consequently gaining status in the group. This was usually achieved by playing the clown and exaggerating known roles. For instance, in a Year Six girl's role-play at Lady Mary school, Charity (F, 11) takes up exaggerated masculine, reactionary adult discourse to make the role of caretaker comical. In response to the role-play problem of children dropping litter she suggests, 'Why don't you make them eat the paper {the others laugh} if they've thrown it around'. She goes on gruffly, 'Well I think my idea was quite good actually {all giggle} (3) they disobey everything you say (.) and you should see wh-what else they do, they even graffiti on the walls'. Her suggested remedy to this problem is for the culprits to be made to 'lick it off'. This causes the other girls much amusement. There were also occasional fantasies of violence in the female role-plays, which appeared to function much like humour in gaining the enthusiasm of the other girls. In a Year Three girls' group, Rebecca (F, 8) repeatedly brings up the theme of murder in their hospital play and a Year Three girls' group discussed in the previous chapters talk vivaciously about 'killing' the boys. Vicks (1990) found in her study that boys appeared to fantasise about violence during drama: my study suggests that girls were equally ready to explore violent themes. The girls' comic play and allusions to violence hardly summon the submissive, conformist, diligent image of primary school girls as suggested by researchers such as Belotti (1975) and Walkerdine, (1990). However, such positions were taken up by girls in *all-female* groups, where the discursive gender dichotomy was not so highly evoked. Girls may also feel more at ease in small, single-sex groups[2]. I found no instances of girls engaging in violent fantasies in the mixed sex role-plays. This could be because such fantasies are incongruous with the discursive constructions of feminine behaviour, which are taken up in opposition to masculinity in the *mixed sex* groups. However, this oppositional construction is less salient in the all-female groups and thus girls are more ready to experiment with violent themes. Similarly the girls clowned far more in the single-sex groups than the mixed – the girls' positionings as sensible and selfless in the mixed sex plays may have meant that fooling would be incongruous with their 'sensible' positions.

Like the female role-plays, many of the male role-plays were very comical. Boys used comedy in both mixed and single-sex role-plays in order to gain status within the group. Like the girls, boys occasionally combined comedy with fantasies of violence. For example, in a Year Three mixed sex group at Lady Mary School, Noel (M, 7) fantasises continually about violent punishment of child litter-droppers and in a Year Six role-play Nima (M, 10), as chef, claims he will chop up any intruding members of the police force and put them in his soup. But where the girls restricted violent fantasies to single-sex groups, boys articulated them in the mixed sex as well as single-sex groups. The articulation of such fantasies is more compatible with constructions of masculinity (silly selfish) than femininity, hence the boys are more able to draw on such narratives when the genders are positioned as opposi-tional during the mixed sex interaction.

The wielding of power derived from high-status roles in single-sex groups

By 'high status roles' I mean the positions of doctor, headteacher and hotel manager. Many girls took up these positions in domineering, totalitarian ways in the single-sex plays, either humorously or seriously. For instance, Zoe (F, 7) becomes tearful with frustration because the other girls in her group do not appear to accept her total power as head-teacher. She bewails their lack of compliance, reminding them, '*I* am the headteacher, you know' (a phrase she often repeats). More humorously, Cally (F, 10, as hotel manager,) yells at her rebellious hotel staff that if they do not comply with her wishes she will chop off their heads. Such comic dictatorship appeared to be a response to the rebelliousness of staff, which was also usually humorous. Comedy was frequently used by girls in single-sex groups to diffuse power in the group by undermining the position of the girl with the highest status role. She in turn sometimes used similar methods to resist such re-positioning, resulting in the comical despotism exemplified by Cally's comment. This was in was a sharp contrast with the mixed sex groups, where the authority of the child with the highest status role was rarely questioned. Although this point is impossible to quantify, there were suggestions in the female role-plays that the power gained from possession of the highest status role was unacceptable to the other girls or was at least a contested issue. This is indicated by the number of comic female role-plays: three of the 11 female plays were totally comical and four more involved a great deal of humour, many of which involved girls with low status roles either specifically challenging or more subtly undermining the authority of the girl holding the high status role. It is also suggested by comments in the role-plays: for example, in a Year Three role-play Lea (F, 7) complains to me of Zoe, 'she, she thinks because she's head teacher she can boss everybody about'. When I suggest that as headteacher Zoe does have some power over decision making, Lea replies, 'You wouldn't like it if *you* were the teacher and she kept = on bossing you about and going Gnn gnnnn'.

Unlike the girls, boys in single-sex boys' groups did not try to under-mine and rebel against high-status, powerful positions. For instance, in a Year Three boys' group Mike (M, 7), in the position of hotel manager, fired his staff one after the other with no resistance from them. Likewise, when hearing of the litter problem, Wesley (M, 7), playing headteacher, thumps his fist on the table and cries, 'This will *not* be tolerated', while the rest of the group sit quietly. This raises the possibility that the power of the high status role was discursively more acceptable when held by a boy than when held by a girl in the single-sex groups, due to the construction of power itself as male (Davies, 1989). Other work has shown how boys accept hierarchies in their interactions with other boys, whereas girls tend to play in smaller groups, and to work co-operatively in the classroom[3]. Perhaps such constructions were reflected in their interaction in the role-play groups. At any rate, constructions of gender appeared to affect power positions in the single sex groups.

Children's constructions of power in the mixed sex groups

The sensible-selfless/silly-selfish dichotomy in the mixed sex groups

Chapter Five discussed how girls took up 'sensible selfless' positions during processes of gender-bonding and maintenance – it was these sensible selfless qualities which separated their symbolic gender culture from the male one. So this position is taken up as one of power by girls. It benefits from the shared approval of other girls, serves to identify one with a female culture and aids female bonding. In addition it theoretically pleases the female teacher as it conforms to her declared wishes (i.e. obedience, conscientiousness, etc) – although we saw that this latter assumption may be misjudged. Researchers such as Walkerdine (1990), Stanworth (1981) and Clarricoates (1980) have demonstrated that in fact teachers not only take these qualities for granted in girls but also find them unattractive and indicative of a repressive lack of individuality.

But while the sensible selfless position was highly regarded and consequently powerful in female interaction, in mixed sex interaction adopting it often precipicated in the abandonment of power to boys. Boys chose 11 of the 15 scenarios, and also gained first choice of role in 11.5 (see Table 1).

Boys gained the most powerful occupational role (doctor, manager, and headteacher) in 9 of the 15 role-play groups. Yet where only one girl who gained the most powerful role got first choice in the group, four boys took the most powerful role as the first choice in the group. Moreover, twice as many girls as boys ended up with last choice and the last choice role was rarely a powerful one. Two of the three most powerful roles (doctor and manager) are traditionally male occupational positions, so it is impossible to tell whether the boys chose these because they seemed traditionally gender-appropriate or because they were the most powerful. Certainly they occasionally used their strong positions as though the two were synonymous, taking on particularly masculine or sexist attitudes and dominating or intimidating the other players. The least male dominated of the three positions was headteacher. The schools' female headteachers were identified as role

Table 1: Children's choices of role in mixed-sex plays

Role Play	role chosen 1st by	role chosen 2nd by	role chosen 3rd by	role chosen last by
1)	boy – chef	girl – manager	boy – rm. service	girl – receptionist
2)	girl – chef	boy – rm. service	boy – manager	girl – receptionist
3)	boy- receptionist	girl – rm. service	girl – chef	boy – manager
4)	boy – chef	girl – receptionist	girl – rm. service	girl – manager
5)	boy – doctor	girl – nurse	girl – receptionist	boy – patient
6)	girl – teacher	girl – playground S*	boy – caretaker	boy – headteacher
7)	boy – doctor	girl – nurse	boy – patient	girl – receptionist
8)	girl – headteacher	boy – teacher	boy – caretaker	girl – playground S
9)	boy – receptionist	boy – manager	girl – chef	girl – rm. service
10)	girl – receptionist	boy – chef	girl – manager	boy – receptionist
11)	boy – manager	boy – chef	girl – receptionist	girl – rm. service
12)	boy – rm. service	boy – manager	girl – chef	girl – receptionist
13)	boy – headteacher	boy – caretaker	girl – teacher	girl – playground S
14)	boy – chef	girl – receptionist	girl – manager	boy – rm. service
15)	boy – caretaker	girl – headteacher	boy – playground S	girl – teacher

(Note the role of receptionist was played by two children in one play).   *playground supervisor models by several children and obviously demonstrated that the job was available to females. The position of headteacher was taken up by the same number of girls as boys. Year Three boys took the most powerful role in five out of six role-plays. The Year Six role-plays were split evenly, with three boys and three girls taking the most powerful roles. While my study is not large enough to draw conclusions from this result, it nevertheless suggests a possibility that the older group draws more upon egalitarian ideas and are less willing to conform to gender stereotyping: this point was borne out by other contrasts between the two age groups (see for example Chapter Three).

This male domination of scenario and role choice in the mixed sex groups appeared at least partially to result from the girls' feminine constructions. Their position as sensible and selfless often meant that they facilitated and accommodated male (silly, selfish) demands or even voluntarily offered the boys control. As a result boys often 'got their own way' at the expense of the girls and dominated the play. Girls' sensible selflessness gained little appreciation in mixed sex interaction. I argue it was because of this sensible selfless construction that, in nine of the thirteen times when a role was left which nobody wanted in mixed sex plays, it was a girl who accepted it. Most of these girls explained their acceptance of the left-over role in sensible-selfless terms: they wanted to save argument, often so that they could get on with their 'work'. For example, Sorrel (F, 10) says that she accepted a role she did not want, even though she did not feel it was fair, 'Because my teacher always says that it's not right to argue with other people'. And Nicole (F, 9) explains she accepted the remaining role because: 'Well if I'd said I wanted to be teacher then there'd be more arguing'. These girls maintained that boys in their place would have argued about the role and so caused trouble: Carlie (F, 10) says she accepted the last role rather than argue with Nima (M, 10) over the one she wanted and claims that had it been the other way around, Nima would have argued. Sandra (F, 9) explains that she did not want the last role of playground supervisor but accepted it to save argument. I questioned her further:

I: ...Do you think that if the *boys* had been left with the last role, just been left with, um, playground supervisor, do you think they would have accepted it, or do you think they would've argued?

S: *Argued*

I: They would've? (.) yeah, why do you think that is?

S: Cos boys argue a lot

I: Yeah (.) why don't *you* argue then?

S: (.) Dunno

Sandra's testimony about the boys' tendency to argue was actually supported by a number of boys. Nima (M, 11) acknowledges that in his group Carlie had to accept the last role of room service attendant but says that in her place he would have refused outright to accept the role, as he would 'never in my dreams be a room attendant'. Likewise, Yain (M, 9) argues that the girl who accepted the last role should have swapped with someone else, but when I ask if he would have been willing to swap with her he replies 'Naahh!' Many children recognised the self-sacrifice of these girls in their interviews but said that they had done the right thing by selflessly averting argument. For example, Ahmed (M, 9) says that although it was unfair that Nicole got left with the remaining role, she was right not to argue because that would have caused trouble. Similarly, Shamin (F, 7) says that Marguerite was right to yield her chosen role to a boy because, 'she wanted to be sensible'. Davies (1989) maintains that gender discourse only recognises female power in the domestic field or as helpers of males. In the mixed sex role-play groups in this study, girls' sensible selfless position as 'helpers of men' (or boys) is shown to become a position of power-lessness. Davies admits that the feminine positions girls take up may render them less powerful. She points out, however, that failing to take up 'properly female' positions may relegate girls to the status of 'not a proper person' and being socially incompetent. Thus by drawing on discourses which position females as caring, selfless and supportive to the male, many girls position themselves as 'properly female' and yet in effect abdicate power in the mixed sex role-play interaction.

So the self-sacrifice of these girls in the mixed sex role-play groups does not position them powerfully. Accepting the low-status roles, and adopting facilitating positions generally reduces their power. But these constructions were not fixed. Having unanimously chosen a hospital scenario, a Year Three mixed sex group went on to choose their roles, and Marguerite (F, 8) immediately chose 'doctor'. A brief argument followed, as one of the boys (Tanvier, M, 7) claimed *he* wanted to be doctor. Marguerite asserted, 'I wanna be the doctor because I'm the boss', but Tanvier persisted and also behaved disruptively, messing about with the other boy in the group. Marguerite eventually capitulated to his petulant demands and resigned herself to playing receptionist in order to get the play started. But the boys continued to fight and mess about and after telling me I should replace the boys with girls because girls are more sensible, Marguerite lost patience and reclaimed her original role choice of doctor. She then assertively took up the part and guided the enacting of the play. So although her sensible-selfless construction lost Marguerite her powerful role initially, when she saw that it had not achieved its aims (i.e. to make the play more successful), she combined 'sensible' with 'assertive' and re-positioned herself to a powerful role within the play.

The last chapter revealed how the female sensible-selfless positions were constructed in opposition to the boys' constructions of their masculinity as silly and selfish (and vice-versa), according to dis-courses of gender duality. That boys used humour more than girls in mixed sex role-play groups could be explained by their construction of male as silly, compared to the construction of females as sensible. I suggest this may also contribute to boys more frequently choosing the role-play scenarios and explain why far fewer boys ended up with the last role in the mixed sex plays. The silly selfish construction allowed boys to be demanding and assertive, while the sensible selfless position led girls to be facilitating and submissive. In the Year Three role-play group described above, Marguerite (F, 7) explained in her subsequent interview that she gave up her role of doctor to placate Tanvier, who would otherwise have ruined the play by being disruptive and 'silly'. Another girl in the play (Shamin, F, 7) comments in her interview that Marguerite did the right thing by doing this so that they could continue with the play, but claims that Tanvier only wanted to be a doctor, 'because he wanted to be better than Marguerite'. This illustrates how the female sensible position accommodates the male selfish position and how the girls may consequently give up any potential power to the boys. Children of both sexes portrayed girls' acceptance of roles which boys refused as normal – the binary opposition of gender positions leads to many girls (albeit in exasperation) facilitating boys' demanding positions.

The children's oppositional gender constructions meant that by accommodating the boys' assertive, demanding behaviour, many girls ended up with the lowest status, least powerful roles. We will see how this sometimes resulted in the girls' subsequent belittlement in the role-plays.

The impact of gender constructions on the taking up of positions of power

Boys took up the highest status role slightly more often than girls in the mixed sex plays. But how differently they played these high status roles was noticeable. Boys appeared far readier to use them in a domineering way and position themselves as controllers of the mixed sex plays, exercising power over the girls and other boy in the role-play group. There were exceptions: later in this chapter we see how a girl took up a powerful role in a domineering manner and how some boys had power exercised over them. However, of the nine times a boy took up the most powerful role, in four they used this position in a domineering way, giving orders and reprimands to the others in the group and behaving in an authoritarian manner. In three more plays boys used their high-status position as one of power, taking a guiding, organisational role. Two girls also used their highest-status roles in this way, and only one girl took up the highest-status role in a domineering manner. The girls and boys who did not take up their high-status roles in powerful or domineering ways did not try to guide or exert authority over the rest of the group.

One Year Three hospital play shows a boy using his high-status role in a domineering manner: Patrick (M, 7), playing doctor, wields his power with confidence and authority, successfully intimidating his co-actors and quashing all opposition to his views. On the one occasion that the receptionist (Angela, F, 7) challenges him, he is swift to remind her of her lesser status with a cutting 'put-down':

A: {threateningly} Doctor, what medicine did you give him?

P: {still looking at Luke} I gave him, antibiotics (.) {dismissive gesture in Angela's direction} now *be* quiet

Thus Patrick uses his powerful position to position Angela as an insignificant subordinate. His final ultimatum to the patient (Luke, M, 7) is: 'now, either you *stay* here, until you get better, or {he drums finger on table for emphasis} you can go to another hospital {he leans back from table} it's *your* choice'. Luke humbly murmurs 'stay here, get better' and Patrick triumphs. It seems that Patrick's strength in his position as having the most respected occupational role in the group cannot be matched and he wields his power advantage to dominate the rest of the group. However, this power was not obviously related to gender: Luke, positioned as powerless, is also a boy. As reported in Chapter Two, Connell (1995) theorises that there are different forms of constructed masculinity and terms the dominant form (which has most cultural status in our society) 'hegemonic masculinity'. Connell, Jordan (1995) and Skelton (1997b) have discussed how this hegemonic masculinity is achieved by boys/men positioning themselves against girls/women *and boys* who have not achieved this form of masculinity. Luke was particularly small and quiet. So it may be that what we are seeing in a mixed sex group such as this, is the boy who has achieved the dominant cultural form of masculinity (Patrick) wielding power over the 'Others' in his group (two girls and a boy).

One boy in particular appeared to construct gender as a source of power. He drew upon gender discourses and combined them with discourses of occupational status to create an unassailable position for himself and to dominate others in the group. Simon (M, 11), playing hotel manager, used his position to intimidate and humiliate the female receptionist (Sabina, F, 10), claiming that she left her bra on the bed in one of the hotel rooms. Recovering from the shock and humiliation, Sabina tried to deny the assertion and retaliate. But Simon was supported by the male chef (Nima, M, 10), who announced that if Sabina complained to the police about this accusation he would chop up any visiting police officers and put them in his soup. Boosted by this support, Simon elaborated enthusiastically that he saw Sabina disappear to the bedroom with one of the Chippendales and that he had caught the incident on film – further mortifying Sabina and rendering her completely unable to retaliate. Thus Simon used his powerful position to produce Sabina (F, 10) as a sexualised object of ridicule. Indeed, he used his gender position and sexist discourse in a similar manner to the boys whom Walkerdine (1981, 1990) observed resisting the power of their teacher (see Chapter One). A position which unashamedly wields power may be more available to boys than girls: boys are able to draw upon male power discourses as well as occupational status discourse to create such positions. Moreover, such positions do not clash with constructions of masculinity. Excerting power over other members of the group (a self*ish*, rather than self*less* position) may be fundamentally incongruous with a construction of femininity as sensible and selfless in opposition to masculinity. It risks rendering the girl concerned *not properly female* (see Davies, 1989).

These examples illustrate how by positioning others as discursively non-powerful or marginalised, one can increase one's own power position. Despite having effectively used his position as male with the highest status role to dominate in the Year Three mixed sex hospital role-play, and its outcome, Patrick (M, 7) is unwilling to accept my suggestion that we conclude the play:

P: {leaning forward and looking down at the table} There's a *bit* more {looks at Luke} cos, you've got to pay your bill for the bed (.) {Angela grins} and electricity {Angela grins and looks at me} (.) now (.) so:o, what floor do you want to go on?

A: {whispers to Luke} Five

L: Err, five

P: Fifth floor (.) ermm, that means you wanna go in the children's department, right?

{Angela and Christine giggle}

L: {laughing} Ye:ah

P: (2) Okay (.) so that's where you'll be staying, until you get better {looks at Luke challengingly}

Patrick positions Luke as childish and ridiculous by informing him he will be staying in the children's ward, so gaining appreciation from the girls (because of the trick he's played on Luke), and further demonstrating his total power. Such positioning of others in discourse so as to increase one's own power position is an inevitable consequence of the struggle for discursive power in interaction. This example also confirms that maleness does not guarantee a powerful position in the group: Patrick used his high status position to dominate Luke as well as the girls.

Most of these instances where children positioned others to increase their own power were extremely subtle and thus it was difficult to tell how those positioned by others as non-powerful or an object of ridicule experienced it. However, Sabina (F, 10) spoke at length about her reaction to being accused of sexual misconduct in her Year Six mixed sex role-play. She explained that she felt shy in the play anyway and that Simon (M, 11) should not have accused her of leaving her bra on a hotel bed, 'because I was a bit, like er- feeling embarrassed'. When he did she 'felt really embarrassed in front of them and you (.) I thought he might never ever say that'. When I ask her whether she thinks Simon would have accused the other boy in the group of sexual misconduct, Sabina says not 'because he's his friend, and he's a male, probably'. When I ask whether she thinks Simon knew it was embarrassing for her, she replies, 'yeah, probably he did think it was embarrassing' and she thinks males do such things to females because, 'they think women aren't so tough as men'. Even in retrospect, at our interview, she cannot think of any effective way to have countered Simon's accusation. His powerful position allowed him to develop his accusations, whereas Sabina's powerless one appeared to undermine any attempts to retaliate. Clearly she found the incident humiliating and was apparently made to feel more powerless because of her lack of resources with which to hit back at him.

The construction of other social issues outweighing gender in terms of power

Many discourses were used to position others and these often outweighed gender in children's constructions of power in the role-play groups. For instance, in a Year Three mixed sex role-play at Lady Mary school, social class discourse was drawn on by Annalea (F,7) in order to belittle the boy playing the role of caretaker and undermine his contributions to the play. She gave him two orders and made disparaging remarks about the menial nature of a caretaker's role, such as, 'And then there'll only be leaves left, and, {laughing} Eddie [care-taker] can sweep them up (.) {the others giggle} cos I'm sure he's used to that'. And in the last chapter we saw how school-orientated concerns with 'bad behaviour' outweighed gender solidarity in a Year Three girls' group. And while in the mixed sex groups the role of caretaker was always chosen by a boy, in an all-boys' group male identification was no longer at issue and social class discourses prevailed, positioning the role of caretaker as menial and distasteful.

Resistance to positionings

According to Foucault (1972, 1980), wherever there is power there is resistance in reaction. Davis (1988) observes that power is a process through which asymmetrical power relations can be not only constructed but also undermined. There were certainly instances of resistance to positionings by other children during the role-plays. For example, when told by the rest of his role-play group he is to play receptionist, Kalpesh (M, 7) gasps, 'Who me?' and when the rest of the group utter a resounding 'Yes you', Kalpesh responds by declaring, 'Then I'm sending everybody out' and the play comes to a standstill again. In a Year Three girls' group, Lea (F, 7) refuses to acknowledge her position of lesser status than the headteacher and is outraged by the headteacher's assertion of power; and in another Year Three girl's group, Tracy (F, 7) vigorously and adamantly refutes Rebecca's (F, 8, playing doctor) attempts to blame her for hospital error. So my findings support Foucault's argument concerning the existence of resistance. However, the overall compliance of the majority of girls in the mixed sex groups suggests that they permit girls fewer resources of resistance than boys. Davis (1988) argues that,

> Members do not have equal access for affecting the outcome of their interaction. Resources are asymmetrically distributed in accordance with structures of domination. (p.89)

Substituting the idea of a hegemonic discourse of gender as oppositional for Davis' 'structures of domination', my findings suggest that children's constructions of femininity, based on the hegemonic discourse of gender dichotomy, may mean that to assertively resist positionings by boys would render girls *non-female*, and thus rob them of social competence. (To be positioned as socially inept could also position them as marginalised and powerless in the interaction.) Moreover, by drawing on combinations of gender and other hegemonic discourses, boys can position themselves so powerfully that they deprive other girls and boys of means of resistance. Hence gender and gender discourse do impact on the resources of power positionings available to children in interaction.

Not constructing gender as a source of power

In six out of 15 mixed sex group role-plays, a girl chose the most powerful (highest status) role. While two of these were actually the last choice, the fact that these six girls took up the positions shows girls as willing to take the highest status role. However, as a noted above, there was a difference between the girls and boys in the way they played these: while the boys frequently used their high status position to dominate the play, only one girl did so in a mixed sex group. It may be no coincidence that this particular girl (Ketchy, F, 9) was much larger than the other children in her class and was very assertive (she informed me that she could beat up all the boys in her class). Ketchy chose the role of headteacher and explained in her interview that she did so because of the power the role afforded: 'you can tell people to do this and you can tell people to do that'. She used her position of authority to dominate the talk and decision-making in the group. I argue that Ketchy did not construct gender as a source of power, but rather drew upon social status discourses to position herself powerfully. However, it could be suggested that, as her school headteacher was female, Ketchy may have drawn on her gender as well as social status to construct her position as powerful. Although she was the only girl in a mixed sex group to use her high-status role in this domineering way, her actions demonstrate the possibility of such positioning being open to girls. And we saw how some boys did not appear able to use their gender to construct themselves powerfully in the plays and were marginalised in the group despite their gender.

Summary

These findings suggest that children's oppositional constructions of gender led to differences in constructions of power in the male and female single-sex groups. Supporting Davies' (1989) hypothesis that children construct power itself as male, it appeared that hierarchical power positions were more frequently resisted and contested in the female groups than the male groups, where power appeared more accepted. Taking up a high-status position in an authoritarian way may be incongruous with children's constructions of femininity. This was more marked in the mixed sex groups, where there was evidence of girls' sensible-selfless constructions leading them to accept more low-status, and consequently less powerful, positions. Boys' constructions, on the other hand, apparently enabled many of them to use their high-status roles to dominate the plays.

In mixed sex interaction, boys' constructions of masculinity became a source of potential power whereas girls' oppositional constructions appeared to become a source of potential powerlessness. On one occasion, gender itself was constructed as a source of power, with a boy combining gender and status to create a powerful position and position others as powerless. Other factors were sometimes found to outweigh gender in their impact on children's interactive power positionings and some children did not construct gender as a source of power. However, the lack of resistance by girls in the mixed sex role-plays raises the possibility that children's oppositional constructions of gender may potentially disadvantage the girls concerning resistance to positionings. So my findings suggest that where they are drawn on in mixed sex interaction, these gender constructions potentially empower the boys and disempower the girls.

Notes

1) For a discussion of the complex, multiple and shifting nature of power positions, see the work of Walkerdine (1990, 1997), or particularly Cohen (1993).

2) Sealey and Knight (1990) and Reay (1990) have shown that girls can be silenced and marginalised in mixed sex discussion by the more assertive and rowdy boys, whereas in single-sex groups they are more confident and vocal.

3) Skelton (1988,1997b) has discussed how boys accept hierarchies in friendship groups and how boys tend to play in large groups, whereas girls have smaller friendship groups and tend to work co-operatively.

CHAPTER 7

THE DISCOURSES DRAWN ON
BY THE CHILDREN

Having come to the conclusion that constructions of gender impacted on the children's power positions during their interaction, I looked back at the interview and role-play data to find out more about the discourses children were drawing on in their constructions. This chapter examines the *mechanisms* behind children's constructions of gender. The range of discourses evident in their talk and how children used them in their arguments are discussed. The second part of the chapter looks at the different types of information and evidence (for example, media, family) which children used in their discussion of gender issues and how much they influenced the children's constructions.

Writers often fail to explain how they have categorised different discourses, with the result that the process can seem arbitrary. So when identifying a particular discourse I try to describe it and provide the grammatical constructions and metaphors by which it was located (see Macnaghten, 1993). I also give an example of the text in which it can be identified. The words 'narrative' and 'discourse' have been used in different ways or interchangeably. But I use 'discourse' to describe the themes which position and describe us and 'narrative' to describe all the ideas and arguments which form the various discourses. For a more extensive explanation of the theory behind my approach, see Francis, 1998b.

After presenting the range of different discourses found in the children's talk about gender issues, their use of these discourses in their arguments are discussed. I also examine their attempts to resist the dominant construction of gender dichotomy.

Identification of different gender discourses

There follows a categorisation and description of the various discourses concerning gender and the narratives supporting them, identified within my data. The general term 'gender discourse' is used by Davies and Banks (1992) to describe all those concerning gender. I have divided these into two groups: 'inequity discourses', which include all those that present the genders as unequal or discriminate unfairly according to gender; and 'equity discourses' (the heading used by Davies and Banks, 1992), including all those which oppose gender discrimination. Other discourses which could overlap with those of gender are also listed.

Inequity discourses

I found two types of gender inequity discourse: that of innate inequality between genders, and an opportunities-should-not-be-equal discourse. The former discourse could be used to construct the genders as different or oppositional. The discourse presented these differences as a source of discrimination.

Innate inequality between genders

Several different narratives were found supporting this discourse in the children's speech. These were:

i) *Male superiority and female inferiority*
Description: unfavourable comparisons of women compared to men, or girls compared to boys and the production of women as inferior. There were three versions of this narrative, which interrelated but were often used in different ways. Firstly, a narrative of female mental inadequacy presented girls as mentally incompetent. For example, Tyrone (M,8) argues that women would not be able to be motor racers because, 'they haven't got a really long, big brain'. Secondly, a narrative of female physical inadequacy and male physical power and ability. Wesley (M,7) uses this to argue that women could not build cars or 'heavy machines', because the work is too heavy and they might get hurt; and Simon (M, 10) says that women cannot play football in mixed teams because men are too 'rough'. Jordan (1995) observed such constructs as evident when boys positioned girls and 'wimpy' boys as Other in school.

Thirdly, the narrative of male superiority, born of the first two, which depict females as inadequate. It elevates masculinity over femininity and consequently ridicules female items. We see it used by Mike (M, 8), when he says Tanvier (M, 7) should play the part of nurse because 'he's a girl'. This narrative is observed by Jordan (1995) to be vital to boys' constructions of superior masculinity.

ii) *Female superiority*
Description: This was similarly based on comparisons between the sexes but produced males as inferior. The narrative tends to present females as mature and sensible and males as immature and badly behaved. For example, Marguerite (F, 7) remarks that I should exchange the boys in their role-play group for girls, as 'girls are more sensible than boys'; and Obie (F, 10) says women are 'more suited' to childcare.

iii) *Stereotypically gendered characteristics and behaviour*
Description: presents a gender-stereotypical picture of the world and draws upon conventional stereotypes to explain differences in behaviour between the genders, both in adult work and in the classroom. Thus it constructs the genders as different. It therefore included generalised comparisons between girls and boys and generalisations about either gender. This narrative overlaps with many of the others but does not necessarily present the differences in gendered behaviour as inherent. For example, Leke (M, 7) says boys and girls are different because 'girls play with dolls and boys play with toys'.

v) *'Battle of the sexes'*
Description: presents the genders as in conflict or competition, thus constructing the genders as in opposition. It is located grammatically when 'the girls' and 'the boys' are presented in antagonism. This included articulations of gender solidarity and strength in numbers. For example, Lynn (F, 7) says there is sexism in the classroom because, 'Boys think they're better than girls and girls think they're better than boys'.

vi) *Female fear*
Description: fear of 'strange men' and possible harm of women and children at their hands. This fear is born out of the cultural materiality

of violence against women (see Soper, 1990). However, the narrative has the effect of discriminating against men and perpetuating the gender dichotomy, as it positions all strange men as potentially harmful and thus constructs the genders as different and in opposition. It was located where children presented men as potentially violent. For instance, Naomi (F, 11) argues that she would employ women to do something other than drive lorries and when I ask her why she explains:

N: Well, it's just a long way for a lady to go on her own and stuff and it might just (.) it wouldn't be as good for a lady to go on her own

I: Right, what might happen?

N: Well (.) it's easier for something to *happen* to a *lady* than a man I think

I: Mmm

N: Cos there are more horrible men in the world

These narratives all present the genders as different. The examples of male superiority, female superiority and 'battle of the sexes' narratives illustrate how innate inequality between genders discourse can also be used to construct the genders as oppositional: the children compare differences between the genders, positioning one gender over the other. So all these narratives support the dominant discursive practice which constructs a gender dichotomy: Davies (1989), and Davies and Banks (1992), refer to this as the 'dominant gender discourse'.

Opportunities should not be equal discourse

This discourse can be seen in many of the examples of narrative above supporting the discourse of innate inequality, for example, when Wesley (M, 7) claims that women should not do heavy work and when Tyrone (M, 8) says that women cannot be motor-racers. It is linked to the discourse of innate inequality, in that claims that opportunities should not be equal between genders were usually based on the supposition that the genders are innately unequal. However, this version does not necessarily state that there are innate gender differences.

Equity discourses:

There were two main equity discourses: one asserting innate equality between the genders and one claiming that *the genders should have equal opportunity.*

Innate equality between genders

Description: positions the genders as the same and equally able. Often used by children to protest at the error and injustice of gender discrimination. The key-words for children drawing on it are 'equal' and 'the same'. For instance, Matthew (M, 11) explains, 'I don't reckon you should be sexist, cos girls, girls can have as many muscles as men' and Emily (F, 10) argues that 'We're all equal'.

Genders should have equal opportunity

Description: argues that gender discrimination is unfair, and that people should be given a chance to prove themselves or to experiment. Based on liberal humanist concepts suggesting that individuals should be allowed to do as they wish and on the concept of 'fairness' so important to children[1]. Unlike the discourse of 'innate equality between genders', equal opportunity discourse does not necessarily argue that women and men can do the same things but is concerned with the rights of the individual to 'try if they want to'. The words 'fair', 'right' and concepts of 'the right to try' often located this narrative. For example, Sally (F, 10) says of discriminatory male builders, 'I think they should give the women a go'.

Discourses which overlapped with those of gender

There were other discourses in children's speech which impacted on or overlapped with those of gender. One was adult-pleasing discourse, as identified by both Davies (1989) and Buckingham (1993) in their research with children. Children occasionally reiterated recognised adult or school values, apparently to impress me or position themselves with me. We can see this overlap between this and gender discourse when Alma (F, 7) expresses disapproval about 'boys always fighting'. There were also discourses of morality or conformity, where tradition or religion were evoked to challenge or support gender equality: Ryan (M, 11) uses such a discourse to support discrimination, arguing that it 'isn't right' for women to be bosses. Michael (M, 7), on the other hand, uses it to oppose discrimination, explaining that 'under God's eye we are *all* brothers and sisters *all* around'.

So children used four different discourses in their constructions of gender as different or not different. And several other discourses and narratives (some directly concerning gender and others which could be applied to it) have been identified as being used to support or oppose the gender dichotomy.

How children draw on discourses

This section examines how children used the discourses just identified in their gender constructions and arguments, as well as the different issues to which they applied them.

The discourse of innate inequality was often produced via the narrative of *male superiority and female inferiority* in children's explanations of gender discrimination in adult work, particularly by boys. The construct of female physical inadequacy was most often used here: almost all the girls who used the narrative of male superiority did so in this way. This narrative was then applied to support the *genders should not have equal opportunities* discourse: we saw in Chapter Three how children claimed that women should not be builders because they are not strong enough or become tired quickly. Women's inferior intellect was used to explain gender-differentiation in adult work by only a tiny minority of children but apparently still exists as a narrative children may have recourse to. These male superiority narratives were also reportedly used in child interaction. For example, Tracy (F, 7) says boys tease girls because 'they think they're more tougher'. My findings described in Chapter Five suggest that these narratives of male superiority are drawn on by boys to aid gender category maintenance and male bonding and to ensure a construction of difference to the girls.

Narratives of *female superiority* were sometimes used by girls in the context of the symbolic gender cultures in the role-plays, apparently aiding female bonding. They were also used when complaining about boys' disruptive classroom behaviour. Some boys also used the narrative of female superiority in this context, to describe girls as better behaved or better at schoolwork. Moreover, this narrative also supported the *genders should not have equal opportunities* discourse when applied to adult work. Sandra (F, 10), for instance, says that women make better teachers and a number of girls and boys argued that women are better at childcare. This narrative was used by more girls than boys – fewer boys drew on this account in comparison to the number of girls who used the narrative of male superiority. This is probably because ideas about male superior strength and prowess are common currency in our society.

The narrative of *stereotypically gendered characteristics and behaviour* was widely drawn on to present a stereotypical picture of males and females in school and adult work. This is hardly surprising considering the nature of my interview questions, which asked children to consider whether boys and girls behaved differently in school, so evoking generalised answers. This narrative was evident in many explanations of differences between the genders. For instance, Denzel (M, 7) informs me that girls want to play hopscotch, where boys want to play football and tennis, and when I ask him why boys would not want to play hop-scotch he replies, 'Because that's – th, they think it's more of a *girl's* game, really'. He uses it to explain differences in behaviour between girls and boys as a consequence of their wish to participate in tradi-tionally gender-appropriate behaviour. This was the most frequently used narrative and was applied most often to explanations of differences in gendered behaviour.

When discussing gender issues in adult work, a number of girls, and fewer boys, drew on a *battle of the sexes* narrative to construct the genders as in opposition. There were claims that male workers would antagonise a woman boss and that she would need to employ women workers to support her. This narrative was mainly utilised by the younger children and it overlapped with that of female fear. For instance, Tracy (F, 7) suggests that a woman boss might be harmed by male workers, and would need female workers to protect her.

So inequity discourse were evident in a wide range of narratives in children's talk about their own lives and adult work. Turning to equity constructions, a number of children drew heavily on the discourse of *innate equality between the sexes*, particularly in talk about gender and adult work. Children expressed frustration and cynicism at male sexism which they perceive to permeate the adult occupational environment. For instance, Johnnie (M, 7) argues, 'I know people just be sexist, I've, I've never been sexist before (.) cos women and men can do exactly the same things'.

The *genders should have equal opportunities* discourse was used by a large proportion of children and often appeared motivated by ideas of *fairness*. Lloyd and Duveen (1992) and Damon (1977) argue that sex role identification generally lessens in children from the age of seven onwards when according to Damon, values of 'fairness' and justice begin to outweigh the need to conform. I found similar numbers of children from *both* age groups appealing to fairness regarding equal opportunities. This pro-equal opportunities discourse is deeply rooted in the discourses of individual rights and democracy which permeate Western culture. Children frequently applied this discourse to gender issues, particularly concerning adult occupation. Emily (F, 10) draws on it to argue that everyone should be allowed to 'have a try'. And Sally (F, 10) comments about men, 'Erm well they, most of them just think women should do the housework (.) n', I don't think it's fair'. Spiros (M, 10) draws on this discourse to argue for freedom of choice concerning behaviour. When asked whether he thinks it acceptable for boys to play with dolls, he replies, 'Err, yeah, yeh it's their life, do what they want'. Many boys were anxious to position themselves as egalitarian via this equal opportunities narrative when referring to the sexism of other males. Johnnie (M, 7) comments on the male builders' attitudes to a female builder, 'They'd start laughing at her and, start being sexist and stuff like that, like if she does something wrong they start saying, Oh you're stupid and all that (.) but, *I* wouldn't mind if I was a builder'. Patrick (M, 7) explains, 'Ermm (.) I think (.) it, I think they would think, it's silly but I don't think it's silly'. Both boys seemed to fear being associated with male sexism – hence their disclaimers.

Thus discourses drawn on in children's egalitarian constructions of gender were as diverse as those drawn on in their discriminatory arguments. Equity narratives were clearly available to children as an alternative to those of gender inequity and were supported by liberal discourses of justice and 'fairness' which children often drew upon.

Discursive resistance

Some children drew on equity discourses to dispute inequity constructions. For instance, Emily (F, 10) describes how boys in her class are
always claiming that men are stronger than women and that women
cannot do the same jobs as men – and responds that the genders are
equal and that everyone should be allowed to do the same thing. Baresh
(M, 8) argues that, 'boys and girls can do the same things', and Sabina
(F, 10) and Tarlika (F, 11) agree that men and women are 'just the
same'. However, their success in challenging the discursive gender
dichotomy via these narratives is debatable. This section examines the
discourses children drew on in resistance to gender-stereotypical or
discriminatory constructions and assesses their level of success in
presenting a challenge to the construction of gender dichotomy.

According to Davies (1989), Davies and Banks (1992) and Jordan
(1995), equity discourses can never effectively combat gender discriminatory discourse because they fail to challenge the assumption of
gender dichotomy. 'Genders should have equal opportunities' discourse simply argues that men and women should have equality of
opportunity *despite* the differences between them, rather than suggesting that the discourse which presents 'men' and 'women' as dichotomous is wrong. Because pro-equal opportunities discourses do not
challenge the fundamental construction of gender as relational, they
can only moderate, rather than challenge, discriminatory constructions.
I found that although 'genders should have equal opportunities' discourses were frequently drawn upon by children in their discussion of
gender in relation to their own lives, causing discursive clashes with
those of gender inequity, these clashes were apparently contained by
the dominant construction of gender dichotomy and failed to challenge
it. For instance, Johnnie (M, 7) articulates equal opportunities discourses throughout his interview but when I ask him whether an
employer would gender differentiate in job allocation he responds,
'Really all the jobs should be for *men*, cos who's gonna look after the
children?'. His 'genders should not have equal opportunities' discourse
contradicts his earlier egalitarian stance. So although 'genders should
have equal opportunities' discourse causes discursive clashes with
those of gender inequity, it appears able to coexist with them in children's constructions. Equal opportunities discourse cannot effectively

combat those of inequity and discrimination, because it does not engage with the deconstruction of the gender dichotomy upon which such inequity narratives are founded.

There were also contradictions to 'innate equality between genders' discourses. For example, Lea (F, 7) asserts, 'girls *can* be what boys do and boys can do what girls do, but some jobs you're not allowed'. Davies and Banks (1992) argue that discourses presenting the genders as equal still fail to challenge the dominant discourse of gender dichotomy because children take up oppositional constructions of gender as part of themselves. This explanation accounts for contradictions such as Lea's. However, I also found some children, particularly 10-11 year old girls, who used 'innate equality between genders' discourse fairly consistently and repeatedly during the research, suggesting that this may be a useful resource taken up by some children to oppose the construction of genders as relational. It can challenge this construction because it presents the genders as having equal ability and rejects gender difference. So this discourse appears to offer some ability oppose the gender dichotomy.

The 'evidence' drawn on by children

Children used evidence from the media and their own lives to support and justify their assertions. Examples and information from wider society peppered the children's talk and supported the discourses they drew on.

How children draw on or are influenced by resources such as books and the media has been looked at in different ways. Particularly in the 1970s and 1980s, Social Learning theorists suggested that the traditional messages of comics, books, television programmes, etc, reinforced stereotypical gender roles. Such theories incorporated the notion of 'role models' with the implication that children and young people emulate examples from the media and wider community. This idea raised the possibility that presenting counter-stereotypical storylines about gender in the media and children's books could provide children with new role models and encourage more egalitarian outlooks in children – such theories have been questioned and branded over-simplistic by many recent writers[2] as discussed in the first chapter.

A poststructuralist/social-constructionist approach looks instead at how children actively take up or reject such storylines and examples to make meaning or use in their own arguments, and how the media reflects social discourses. Davies (1989) investigated children's interpretation of 'feminist fairy tales'. Gonick (1997) investigated young women's use of teen magazines in their construction of gender identity. Both maintain that children draw on known discourses embedded in storylines to reference their own construction of identity. Davies goes no further than this, but Gonick does appear to suggest that the teen magazines *reinforce* a traditional construction of femininity. However, both writers agree that traditional discourses within storylines can be resisted by drawing on alternative discourses (see Foucault, 1980).

I wanted to look at the types of information resources children drew upon and how these were used in their discussion of gender issues. I found four different types of resource being drawn on in children's discussion of gender:

> Family, wider community, anecdotal evidence and media.

Family

When discussing gender issues, children often cited their parents as examples. This was usually to show *either* that men and women differ or do separate jobs; or to show the opposite, that men and women are the same or can do jobs traditionally performed by the opposite sex. The former use was most common, possibly because children felt they needed to provide justification for their gender-discriminatory constructs. For example, Claudine (F, 7) explains that men would not be able to look after old people because they cannot cook:

I: Ah (.) what if he could cook? cos some men [can, can't they?

C: [My dad can't cook

I: Some men can though,   [can't they?

C: [He only cooks, um, sausage and bacon,

and um, puts some toast- he does all them things, for breakfast=

I: Right

C: =And my mum has to do all the cooking

I: Right (.) but some men are good cooks, aren't they? (.) {she nods} and can
     they look after old people?

C: (.) It wouldn't be right

I: It would just look *strange*

Similarly, Maddie (F, 7) argues that women are better than men at
cleaning, explaining her father's inadequacy in this department: 'Wh-
when my dad comes in he, he does the hoovering and he thinks that's
it, the whole house is clean but my mum does the dusting, and the
washing up'. Sonia (F, 7) says that women cannot drive well enough to
be lorry drivers because her mother has not yet learnt to drive and goes
on to say that men cannot be childcarers:

S: Because, well my daddy, um well when I was little, he, he couldn't hold me,
     whenever my mum asked him to hold me he kept dropping me,
     [he couldn't do it

I: ˙[Really? oh *dear*

S: So that's why I wouldn't ask a man to do it

Reema (F, 9) appears to have her argument revoked by her own
example: having argued that her father's inability at housework shows
that men cannot do it, she goes on to claim that men cannot cook either:

R: Like, my mum can cook, my dad can't

I: Mm (.) right (.) but do you think that men *can't* cook, or if they want to they
     can?

R: Um, men can't cook, but *my* dad can cook

I: Your dad can cook? so some men can cook? {she nods} yeah

R: Mmm

Other children used their parents as evidence that men and women can
perform the same jobs and tasks. For instance Rebecca (F, 8) decries
traditional gender roles: 'Because they say women are too feminine an'
all this stuff an' women have to stay at home an' do the housework =
and men, men are the best so they 'ave to go out and do loads of things,

lots of work, and they're not allowed to stay at home and do the house-work- what's the matter with *that*? a man could stay home and do the housework, an' do the dinner, an' look after the baby, *my* dad does'. Johnnie (M, 7) argues that traditional gender roles can be reversed in the home: 'Well, yeh- my mum used to go out to work, and my dad used to pick me up from school, and my dad has to take me to school when my mum's ill'. In this case it appears that his father's unemployment may have affected gender roles at home, and consequently supplied Johnnie with evidence of the possibility of non-traditional gender roles. Likewise, Baresh (M, 8) maintains that it is acceptable for a woman to go out to work while her husband cares for the children: 'Yes, y'know my mum, she had to go to work before- when she used to go to work my dad used to look after me and my sisters when we were small, cos he didn't have no work then'. So children used parents as evidence both in constructions of genders as different, and of genders as not different.

Some children chose future occupations in line with those of their parents. For example, Johnnie (M, 7) wanted to play the chef in the role-play because his father 'was a chef in GMTV' and Sarah (F, 8) says she wants to work in Safeways and 'be a mum', which is what her mother does. But as noted in Chapter Three, it is unlikely that children will follow the career paths they chose at primary school. However, that children suggest work in the same employment as their parents illustrates how children draw on information and examples from their social surroundings to refer to their own lives and thoughts.

Parents, then, are sources of information for children, particularly concerning adult life about which the children themselves have no experience. I suggest this explains why parents were so often referred to as examples or justifications when children discussed gender and adult occupation (eighteen children used parents as examples in this manner). They are a source of evidence for children to draw upon in discussion of gender issues.

Wider community

Children also cited people in their own experience other than family members in their discussions – people they knew or had observed. For example, when I ask Richard (M, 10) whether he would employ a male childcarer he replies, 'Ye:eah, I've got, I'm using a childcarer who's a man'. Real life examples from school were frequently mentioned, for instance Rafic (M, 9) explains that he chose the role of caretaker, 'cos, I like the way the caretaker, like, has got a lot of jobs to do, I like the jobs he does, and I, when he does the jobs, he like, not too hard, and he's got a lot of friends, and everyone wants to help'. Similarly Yain (M, 10) says that he wanted to be headteacher because he likes the one at their school: 'I like being the headmaster (.) head*mistress*, cos she, when you get into trouble, she doesn't really *shout* (.) she just says Don't do it again, and things'; and Reema (F, 9) refers to the male teacher in her school when she says men make as good teachers as women.

Having *seen* something appeared to carry considerable importance for children when using evidence or evaluating issues. Shofic (M, 7) argues that women cannot be builders because he has never seen a woman builder, although they can be decorators because, 'I've seen a lady *paint*'. Catia (F, 8) observes that boys claim to be stronger than girls but argues, 'I 'ave seen a girl who's stronger than a boy, so I think it's not true'. Likewise, Michael (M, 7) claims that women can be builders, 'Cos I've seen um many women do building ... sometimes, I see more women than men work on building sites'. This emphasis on visual observation may be due to their relative lack of experience in the world: having *observed* or witnessed something changes a child's assertion or theory to a substantial reality. Moreover, not having observed something means that its non-existence remains a possibility.

Anecdotal evidence

So far the data has shown children using real life examples gained first-hand, but occasionally children used anecdotal evidence as a resource – that is, information reportedly gathered by or given to the children by some outsider. For example, Somina (F, 11) argues against employing male childcarers, relating that a woman she knows hired a male childcarer and he mistreated the baby. And Graham (M, 10) argues that a woman builder would be incompetent in the following way:

G: *Useless*

I: Women, or-? woman builders?

G: Yep (.) there was one lady she was building, helping the men over at Six Acres, she was just trying to, help 'em pick up bricks and she kept dropping 'em, and breaking 'em, they just 'ad to keep paying out more and more money (.) for more bricks

I: Who, who told you this then?

G: (.) Oh loads of children standing there *watching*

Media

Another commonly used resource was the media, drawn on frequently by children as evidence in their discussion of many issues, including gender. Kasheef (M, 10) explains his assertion that some women are better than men at designing computer games:

I: Do you think that a woman can be a games designer or a graphic designer?

K: A woman can be

I: Yeah

K: Sometimes they're *better*

I: Do you think?

K: Sometimes they are, I've got a graphics magazine at home and they say women make most of the games

I: Do they?

K: Most of the good games

I: That's interesting, I didn't know that

K: Well yeah, thass, women make most of the good games

While Kasheef's reported source of evidence is a graphics magazine, the most frequently drawn upon media source was television. Television has been cited as a major agent of sex-role socialisation (Frueh and McGhee, 1975) but researchers such as Durkin (1985) and Gunter and McAleer (1990) argue that there is little evidence to suggest that television directly 'socialises' children. Durkin maintains, rather, that children use television as a source of information about sex-roles. As programme material is often sexist, it may in some cases reinforce stereotypes which children have already adopted. Buckingham (1993) shows how children use talk about television in their interactive constructions and refer to the contents of television programmes in different ways depending on who they are speaking to. I found that children used television as a source of information when discussing gender issues but seemed to use this information to justify their own assertions. Information drawn on from the media sometimes concerned gender issues directly and at other times was of a more general nature but was alluded to in children's discussions of gender. Kasheef (M, 10) provides an example of the latter when he explains that he would not employ a male childcarer because he had watched an Esther Ranzen programme about a man who abused children. Likewise, Charity (F, 11) explains that she knows there are women lorry drivers because she has seen 'lots' of them on television game shows; Leke (M, 7) uses the example of the female 'gladiators' to demonstrate that women are strong; and similarly Ryan (M, 8) maintains that some strong women can be builders, because, 'there's this really big muscley girl in the newspaper'.

Other children referred to incidents where films or television programmes had directly addressed gender issues. Sorrel (F, 10) explains that she would employ a male childcarer, as it would be funny, 'cos on this programme, this film *Look Who's Talking* there's a very funny man in it' (the *Look Who's Talking* films involve John Travolta taking a share in childcare). And Sally (F, 10) tells me that she wishes to become a fire-fighter, inspired by the woman fire-fighter on the television series *London's Burning*. Discussing gender and adult work, Patrick (M, 7) explains his expectation of gender discrimination on the part of male builders in response to a woman boss like this:

P: Um, cos (.) y'know, in, um television comedies, er girls, and er boys are saying that we can beat them we can beat them, when actually the girls do

I: Right, so you think there's a bit of competition between the two (.) between men and women?

P: Yeh

I: What sort of TV shows are those?

P: Erm, Saved by the Bell (.) The Cosby Show (.)

Patrick can justify his claim that men would not want a female boss by drawing on a similar theme in comedy television shows to support his argument. He may or may not believe that the comedy shows accurately represent real life – the fact remains that Patrick can recognise the 'battle of the sexes' narrative and can draw on and apply the theme to a different situation outside his personal experience.

Buckingham (1993) reports that children follow the Australian soap operas avidly and my study confirmed that (particularly regarding *Neighbours*). Children seem to become very involved in these scripts of social relations, using them perhaps for information concerning adult relationships or perhaps as fantasies (like Walkerdine, 1990, suggests girls use comic and 'school story' scripts). I was researching in schools at a time when the *Neighbours* storyline was exploring a gender and adult work issue: the female character, Beth, had just begun work on a building site and had consequently become a victim of sexist ridicule from the male builders around her (whom Beth proves wrong, by remaining undaunted and demonstrating her ability). This story-line was often referred to in the children's interviews concerning the employment of a woman builder and the possible reactions of her male fellows. For example, I asked Jade (F, 7) what male builders would think of a female builder:

J: (2) Think she- (.) oh, on Neighbours *Beth* was working on a building and um all these men were all *jealous* of her

I: Mmm, do you think that would happen in real life?

J: Yeah

I: Yeah, and what would she do about it?

J: She would have to tell the boss about it

I: Yes, and do you think the boss would listen?

J: (.) Well (2) I think he would listen to both

Replying to the same question, Chantelle (F, 7) observes, 'It's like in
Neighbours when Beth was trying to (.) Beth's one they didn't like her,
but they, they 'ad to get used to the idea'. Junior (M, 10) says that he
thinks men and women can do all the same jobs, 'cos in Neighbours,
erm, Beth does what-do-you-call-it? (.) erm, house thing'. Tracy (F, 7)
alludes to another *Neighbours* storyline (in which the female character
Annaleas, asked by a couple to look after their baby, leaves it alone
while she goes out to see someone – to the consternation of the couple,
who return to discover the baby alone), when asked whether she would
employ a male childcarer:

I: Would you pay a man to look after it [the child]?

T: Of course

I: You would, you think men are good at childcare?

T: Be*cause*, in Neighbours, err, anyway, this girl (.) erm, her boyfriend was,
     was gonna go out, and er the girl that knew, the mum, yeah? she had the
     baby, and she asked some other girls to look after it (.) and, she's wanted
     to see someone, yeah? She *hasn't* took the baby,   [she's left it in=

I: [Oh I see, yeah

T: =the cot, an' she's gone, an' then the two people have to come back an'
     they've seen, the baby there, *screaming* (.) an' the girl ain't there

I: So you think a man would be just as   [good?

T: [Yeah, a man

So the media provided a resource for children concerning gender
categories and issues and the storylines of television programmes
seemed to engage children's imagination regarding these issues. Again,
examples from the media were used to construct genders as different
and as *not* different. What, then, is the impact of these resources on
children's constructions of gender?

Children's rejection of evidence concerning gender

We can see from the data presented in this chapter that resources of
observed, reported and media examples were frequently drawn on in
the children's discussions of gender issues, yet were used discursively
(i.e. as evidence to support a particular discourse). Although some chil-

dren drew on such examples to support their arguments, actively contested real life and media examples. Lesley (F, 7) claims that men cannot be nurses, as, 'Thassa woman's job', so I present her with a counter-stereotype:

I: Have you seen Casualty?

L: Yeah, about a thousand times

I: You get men nurses on there look (.) there are men nurses and women doctors, {Leslie laughs} there are

L: Men nurses! {laughs again}

Lesley refuses to accept both the counter-stereotype and my own information. It appears that media examples are only effective if supported by discourse: in this case, the counter-stereotyping example of the male nurses on *Casualty* is passed off, as it is not strong enough to challenge the dominant inequity discourse of male inability at such work. Durkin (1985) found that short-term exposure to counter-stereotyping on television did not necessarily make an impact on children's opinions unless it was supported by discussion, as counter-stereotypes are unsupported by the dominant perspective of society (and television) at large. Davies (1989) observes that simple counter-stereotyping role models and equal opportunities schemes cannot be enough to undo gender discourses which children have taken up *as part of themselves*. Thus besides Lesley's rejection of male nurses, there were other incidents in my research where children explicitly rejected media counter-stereotypes. Characters representing media counter-stereotypes are fictional and while many children *did* use such fictional characters as evidence in egalitarian arguments, it was easy for children to reject these as 'make-believe' in absence of real-life examples to support them. Johnnie (M, 7) actively rejects the character *Mrs. Plug the Plumber* as a legitimate example of anti-gender stereotyping:

I: Would you employ women to build your house?

J: Nah

I: No, why not?

J: Cos you can't get women plumbers, only Mrs. Plug the Plumber

I: {laughs} Only Mrs. Plug the Plumber?

J: Yes

I: But do you think if she exists that some women might in real life?

J: Mm (.) nah

I: No? How come?

J: Because um, Mrs. Plug the Plumber is only a book.

It seems that Walkerdine (1997) is correct when she argues that books such as *Mrs. Plug the Plumber* are far too tokenistic to challenge children's participation in the dominant construction of genders as relational. Amrish (M, 10) brings up the 'Beth off Neighbours' incident again, but to demonstrate his view that women *cannot* be builders:

I: What about umm, building, could women be builders in your company?

A: Mmm, no

I: No? why not?

A: Well, I saw, Neighbours, yeah?   [err, when err, when the man told

      that lady to do the building, but=

I: [Mmm (2) that was Beth, wasn't it?

A: Yeah

I: Mm

A: But err, and then er, all the crowd, they said that women can't be err, be builders

I: But she still did it, didn't she?

A: Mm

I: So do you think she could- if she managed to do it, do you think other women

      could?

A: (.) Little bit

Amrish uses the male crowd's objection to Beth to affirm his view that women should not be builders but he gets stuck when I use the example as the programme makers intended: hence he ends up unwillingly conceding the possibility of women conducting building work. Noel (M, 7) is more decided still in his refutal of this incident. When he claims that women cannot be builders I bring up the *Neighbours* story-line:

I: What about Beth in Neighbours, cos Beth is a builder isn't she, in Neighbours, do   [you think=

N: [Mmm

I: =that's not real, or=

N: No, it's not real

I: You think in real life she couldn't be?

N: Dunno.. [how?] she could be

I: She couldn't?

N: No

These examples suggest that some attempts at education through counter-stereotyping may be ineffective, because they fail to disrupt dominant inequity discourses. However, other evidence presented here also shows how different children drew on these counter-stereotypes to support egalitarian statements. Moreover, Troyna and Hatcher (1992) have shown how children can choose to take up discourses which their parents do not use. They show examples of children with racist parents who refute their parents' constructions and children with egalitarian parents who still articulate racist discourse. My study revealed not only these children who rejected anti-sexist example but also a number of children who discounted sexist example. For instance, Sorrel (F, 10) notes:

S: {laughing} My dad says that women are stupid drivers

I: {laughs} Did he?

S: Cos sometimes, when he's driving, like, say he's behind this woman driver, he'll shout at them 'n' beep his horn at them

I: Does he? Do you think that's right or not?

S: No, because he doesn't give the person a chance

Thus she recognises her father's construction but dismisses it. Likewise Vivek (M, 10) explains that his father thinks women 'muck up work' but he himself thinks this unfair because, 'some women have got skills'; and when I ask whether men and women are better at certain jobs, Natasha (F, 10) replies that her mother is a better cook than her father but then rejects this saying, 'I suppose they're all the same really... If they've had prac- practice at it, yeah, they can do anything'. Thus where counter-stereotyping resources are not always taken up by children, stereotypical resources can be discounted too.

Summary

This chapter has demonstrated the variety of discourses and resources which are actively used by children in their constructions of gender and adult occupation. Equity narratives were used to resist those of gender inequity and discrimination but did not necessarily challenge the dominant discourse which perpetuates such discriminatory constructions. As a consequence these equity narratives were often limited to causing discursive contradictions in children's talk about gender. However, there was some evidence of children successfully drawing on the discourse of innate equality between genders to position the genders as the same.

That children were provided with evidence which they applied to gender issues via their access to the media and different examples from family and the wider community, suggests that access to social resources could affect their gender discourse. The way in which children often discounted both counter-stereotyping and traditional information demonstrates that resources are used to support the particular discourse they are using. Information is certainly not simply uncontestedly consumed, as implied by social learning theory. These findings show that real life, anecdotal and media examples do not determine social roles: rather, children draw flexibly on different resources of outside information, in different ways, to support whichever discourse they are drawing upon.

The findings suggest that providing children with counter-stereotypical literature and information is unlikely to be sufficient to break down traditional stereotypes and ideas supporting the dual roles of the genders. Such counter-stereotypical material may be rejected as it is too superficial to counter dominant gender discourses, in which children may have deep investments of identity and desire. However, that many children did draw on such counter-stereotypes as evidence when using equity discourse indicates that such information can provide a useful resource. Certainly such material should not be dismissed out of hand. The next, final chapter addresses some of the implications of the findings of this book for teaching practice and attempts to suggest some positive ways in which equity teaching could be made effective.

Notes

1) Piaget (1964) has shown how important concepts of 'fairness' are to children, particularly in the later primary years. The work of Damon (1977) and Hutchings (1990) supports this, demonstrating that fairness is one of the strongest values for primary school children.

2) See, for example, Connell (1995) and Davies (1989) for a criticism of social learning theory.

CHAPTER 8

CLASSROOM PRACTICE AND THE GENDER DICHOTOMY

This final chapter summarises the findings of my research and discusses their implications for children's futures. Concluding that the gender dichotomy must be deconstructed in order to allow children (and adults) a greater variety of choices in their constructions of their own behaviour, I suggest possible ways in which teachers can help bring about change through classroom practice.

The implications of the findings

This book demonstrates how, although equal opportunities discourse has obviously had an impact on children's constructions of gender, it is the dominant discourse of gender dichotomy which children largely draw upon as the foundation of their own constructed gender identities. Before discussing the gender dichotomy, a brief consideration is needed of children's use of equal opportunities discourse.

Equal opportunities discourse was drawn on frequently by children in their discussion of gender and adult work. As a result their interview responses appeared far more egalitarian than have children's responses to previous research (see Chapter Three). Certainly such equal opportunities discourse did not seem so widely available when I attended primary school twenty years ago. Girls now seemed far more aware of the world as a harsh environment where they would be reliant on their own resourcefulness and ability. Previous research found that girls saw themselves in the future as being secondary earners, who would give up work to look after children while their husbands supported the family[1]. However, the girls in my study were full of talk about the unreliability of men and the importance of being able to find work. The fact that I was conducting research at the height of recession in 1993/ 1994 and that many of the children's fathers were unemployed, will have also made an impact on children's constructions. The changing economic environment influences the discourses available to children (and adults). While mothers might of necessity have taken on the bread-winning role and fathers child care they nonetheless demonstrate to their children that such roles are open to women and men. As already noted, the lesser support for the idea of a male child-carer compared to children's endorsement of women builders and lorry drivers suggests that equal opportunities discourse has focused on women's ability to perform traditionally male jobs, rather than the other way around. But here the discourse of female/ child fear of 'strange men' may also be at work, especially considering the high media focus on paedophilia in the 1990s.

My main argument concerns children's construction of their own gender identities through a dominant discourse of gender dichotomy which positions the genders as relational. Like Davies (1989, 1993) I have shown that in processes of gender category maintenance children take up visual signs of their gender, which can be behavioural as well as physical (the types of games you play, as well as the clothes you wear). I argue that these gender category maintenance processes, coupled with primary school-centred educational discourse, culminate in children constructing the genders as oppositional in the classroom. This oppositional construction produces a dichotomous construction of girls as sensible and selfless and boys as silly and selfish. This construction, though not taken up in any uniform or consistent way by children, did serve to create symbolic gender cultures during their interaction. Here I maintain that the 'post-modern modern' combination of feminist and post-structuralist approaches in my work has proved fruitful. At the beginning of this book I explained that I sought to ground discourse analysis in social experience in an attempt to analyse power inequalities. My findings show that such power inequalities can result from the use of gender discourse (and in particular, from the resulting dichotomous construction of the genders). While girls' sensible selfless positions could be used as a source of power in the single-sex role-play groups, we saw how in the mixed sex groups the sensible selfless position often led girls to yield power to the boys. The most powerful boys were then able to draw on their construction of masculinity as silly and selfish to dominate the play and the other members of the group. So although power is discursively produced and the minutiae of different factors contributing to power positioning cannot be analysed independently, broader structural inequalities can. Children's constructions of gender and use of gender discourse often impacted on their interactive power positions in this study. As discourses of gender are common throughout British society and are not specific to schools, it is reasonable to expect that one might find similar results in other schools (though discourses available due to socio-economic background or ethnicity would differ from school to school, and might impact on gender discourse). Further research would be needed to examine this hypothesis.

Although my findings have focused on the loss of girls' power in mixed sex interaction due to children's construction of the genders as oppositional, the analysis of these oppositional constructions may also have implications for the contemporary debate on boys' educational 'failure'. Yates (1997) and Weiner *et al* (1997) have pointed out that boys are actually improving their educational results – but that girls have been improving more dramatically over the last twenty years. And Yates observes that twenty years ago, just as now, the rates for boys being excluded or sent to special needs classes were far higher than those of girls, – their comparative 'failure' is not an entirely new phenomenon. Girls are certainly catching up rapidly with boys in even the most traditionally masculine subjects (such as mathematics) and have overtaken them in others at GCSE and 'A' level. The British heavy industrial base involving traditionally masculine work continues to shrink while the service industry grows and examination results are increasingly required for employment in a competitive and insecure job market. The comparative lack of success of males at communicative studies such as English and foreign languages and the greater number of young men leaving the education system without qualifications should perhaps be examined more fully.

The silly selfish construction taken up by many boys in my study does not rest comfortably in a school culture where obedience, diligence, and respect for the teacher are expected. Skelton (1997b) shows how one of the marks of the achievement of hegemonic masculinity amongst the working-class boys in her study was to 'get one over' the teacher. Previous feminist studies have shown that disruptiveness in boys is often tolerated by teachers and even constructed as positive – it shows individuality and character![2] However, my findings do raise the possibility that in constructing themselves in opposition to the feminine sensible selfless position, boys may also be constructing themselves as against the school culture. Walkerdine (1988, 1990) has shown how girls' obedience and diligence has been positioned as repressive in the 'child-centred' educational discourses originating in Piagetian cognitive psychology. But since the late 1980s government educational policy has reflected a return to the discourse of 'the basics' (the three 'R's, well-presented coursework and exam success). Boys' constructions of masculinity may not sit so easily with this discourse.

Girls have traditionally been more successful than boys at primary level. To test my hypothesis that dominant gender constructions impact on levels of educational success I would have to examine whether the constructions of gender I found in the primary school are maintained amongst secondary school pupils. Skelton (1997b) notes that although much British academic research on boys has built upon feminist work, many reports and information packs provided to schools do not draw on feminist research. Some of these tend to imply that girls have acquired their success at the expense of boys and that now it is boys who should have extra help (see Yates, 1997). As I write this, I have just watched our current education minister talking on television about a new homework club scheme where children can do school work in football clubs. It was quite clear that this was designed to persuade boys to engage in schoolwork, rather than encourage girls to become involved in football! This is surely problematic – are not girls once again being told that their learning needs are less important than boys'? Girls will learn in the usual ways, while boys need special provision and incentives. My findings would have very different implications for boys, suggesting that it is boys' construction of masculinity which needs deconstructing. (Ironically, I have incidentally shown how football seems to play a part in boy's construction of hegemonic masculinity). Indeed, the whole relational gender dichotomy needs deconstructing so that girls are not dominated in classroom interaction and boys and girls are not constructed so differently that their constructions affect their levels of educational success.

A further aspect of their lives affected by the gender dichotomy may be children's choice of future occupation, at primary school and in the future. The children's choices of occupation reported in Chapter Three largely reflected a binary dichotomy of arts/vocational jobs as female and science/competitive jobs as male. While Kelly's (1989) work demonstrates that the occupations children chose are unlikely to be those they actually pursue after leaving school, the binary dichotomy constructed in children's choices is reflected in the worlds of higher education and adult work. The arts/female science/male dualism is vividly illustrated in students' choices of university courses. Far more men take up science and engineering degrees, and women humanities degrees (Thomas, 1990). And in the jobs market women tend to be concentrated in the service industry and vocational occupations, while more men work in technical industry. Clearly, the discourse of gender dichotomy is reflected in these social trends. After leaving school, people continue to make choices about their lives based on their gendered constructions of identity. The discourse of gender dichotomy is also evident in the assumptions that women should necessarily be primary childcarers, translated into workplace practice over maternity/paternity leave. But crucially, because 'masculine' traits tend to be ascribed more value than 'feminine' aspects in this dichotomy, female childcare is positioned as less valuable than male breadwinning. Again, the gender dichotomy needs to be challenged if we are to see a change in such assumptions.

The role of schools

Children should be able to take up positions which are gentle and caring or adventurous and assertive without being constructed as strange or erroneous. The constructions of both masculinity and femininity have positive and negative aspects. Children should be able to explore, for instance, bravery and tenderness, and have both valued irrespective of their gender. It is only through a dismantling of the gender dichotomy which assigns these traits to one gender or the other and which children take up as fundamental to their gender identities, that such freedom and flexibility could be achieved. Davies (1989) argues that children should be free to take up positions normally associated with the other sex and maintains that literature and information which challenge the gender dichotomy can provide children with new possibilities with which to do so. She suggests that the school has a role to play in this – and here we come to teachers. For what I (like Davies) am suggesting is that teachers and classroom practice can contribute to the deconstruction of traditionally gendered positions among children. But this possibility raises a number of problematic issues. How could one teach gender deconstruction; would it be ethical; how would such teaching fit into the national curriculum; and importantly, do we *want* to deconstruct the gender dichotomy?

The gender dichotomy and desire

One of the main problems for feminist teachers and academics is that they, like the students they teach, have much invested in the discourse of gender dichotomy. This applies equally (or perhaps even more) to men, but here I am writing from my own female experience and thinking mainly of our construction of notions of beauty and romance. Feminist researchers have built up a large body of work on the pressure and also the desire to conform to Western notions of female beauty and on the seductive attraction of romantic narratives[2]. The narratives of heterosexual romance, where man rescues woman and transforms her life for the better, have been shown by Walkerdine (1990; 1997) and McRobbie (1978) to permeate Western culture and occupy a special place in the lives of women. Fairy stories and girls' magazines are the commonest examples. Storylines vary only slightly across a common theme: a girl should be good, beautiful, kind and patient, and one day a handsome prince or Mr. Right will arrive and whisk her a way to a glamorous, passionate, happy life. She is passive: she waits. The active dashing man does just that – he dashes. Heroes and heroines have very different qualities in Western culture. In her book *The Cinderella Complex* (1982) Collette Dowling argues that these fantasies have been the bane of women and the women's movement: however strong and assertive women are, however successful in their careers, they run the risk of succumbing to this narrative immediately a man appears on the scene. Becoming passive and reliant on him, they are inevitably let down, as men rarely turn out to be princes. And princes rarely turn out to be nice. Yet the seductive notion of an easy yet fulfilled life, with a man providing love, protection, comfort and passion, and where our virtue and patient charm is recognised and rewarded, remains terribly appealing.

In her fascinating book *Daddy's Girl* (1997), Valerie Walkerdine explores the impact of these narratives of romantic rescue and escape on the lives of working class girls. Her book illustrates how these narratives can interpreted differently by different social groups. She also shows how for working class girls such fantasies are linked not just with romance but also with material wealth – the fantasy of being 'taken away from all this' to a glamorous, easy world. Her analysis is far more complex, probing how girls are positioned and construct themselves within discourses of romance, 'rags-to-riches' stardom, and female sexuality (which is why I wish she had provided a more rigorous and detailed explanation of the constitution of different social classes in the 1990s and the impact of factors such as ethnicity).

But for me the most useful aspect of her book is the discussion of how such fantasies can have liberating and empowering aspects as well as oppressive ones. In a society where these discourses of female beauty and romance predominate, doesn't it feel great to believe that one has achieved that notion of beauty? As male eyes rest admiringly upon you, don't you feel a sense of power? I was glad to read Walkerdine's 'confession' of her love for glamour and dressing up, because I enjoy them so much too. Being attractive to men (and to women – and to myself – though this is also measured on heterosexual notions of beauty) remains important to me, a heterosexual woman. The interest of attractive men remains flattering and makes an important contribution to how I feel about myself. It is like the old joke about a feminist who passes a group of builders regularly. Each time she is greeted by their whistles and hoots of objectifying appreciation and returns irate expletives. But when one day they don't whistle she is upset and wonders what is wrong with her. Thus do aspects of our constructions of ourselves become deeply embedded in dominant gender discourses.

In her work with groups of white secondary school girls Valerie Hey (1997) observes this 'powerful attraction to heterosexuality's cultural forms' (p.119). She discusses how one girl talks of her enjoyment in being viewed as attractive (though she also talks of the dangers such positioning entails, such as being viewed as a 'slag'). The girl's feminist friend disapproves of this and in their talk over the issue the two seem to be coming from wholly polarised positions. Hey makes the important point that puritanical feminist discourses are unable to recognise the pleasure and power of being constructed as a desirable girl. Much self-esteem can be derived from feeling attractive, but as I have discussed and as Hey points out, it is such cultural practices of heterosexuality that have at times been seen by feminists as undermining the feminist project. I think it is vital that we recognise the investments of pleasure, desire and power that many women and girls have in the narratives of female beauty and heterosexual romance. It will be impossible to help children to challenge the gender dichotomy (which such discourses build from) without an understanding of such investments – and indeed, this recognition is important to enable us to understand the ways in which the gender dichotomy impacts upon our own lives.

Davies (1989) argues that, for young children, taking up gendered traits can be integral to their construction of themselves as socially competent. In her book *Shards of Glass* (1993) she discusses the danger and awfulness of being relegated to the gender margins, which can involve exclusion and feelings of social inadequacy. If we remember how in Chapter Two Leke explained that playing with Barbies was out of the question however much he wanted to, we begin to see how rigid the gender delineation can be in children's minds and how much they have invested in its maintenance. Add to this the danger involved in challenging the gender dichotomy – and our own attachment to it. It is not just that we have our own investments in it but also that the discursive mechanisms of the dichotomy are embedded in our lives and we reproduce them unthinkingly, from habit. Davies (1993) relays instances where her fellow researcher and the class teacher talk and respond to children in terms of the dominant gender dichotomy while conducting the research on it. Her work also illuminates the difficulty in trying to disrupt the investments of desire and power embedded in discourse and desire for known storylines.

But maybe both genders can be encouraged to invest in other narratives? The idea of being desired by a powerful Other and taken to lead a passive but protected, glamorous life where a partner lavishes you with affection and material goods is understandably appealing. As Walkerdine suggests, it may have particular appeal to girls from working class backgrounds but surely we could all fantasise about the idea, particularly when we are feeling ground down by the pressures of our lives? And by all I mean *all*. Surely this fantasy could be just as appealing to males? It sits in opposition to the dominant construction of hegemonic masculinity as active and independent (and the provider rather than the provided-for; protector rather than protected) but men appear to be becoming gradually less hostile to the notion of their female partners earning more than they do. Men are usually pleased by presents and romantic gestures from their partners; it is just less culturally acceptable for them to expect such spoiling. Likewise, though only a fragment of the size of the women's, the men's fashion industry is gradually growing. I enjoy dressing up and wearing make-up (though I certainly do not think women should be *expected* to) – so why shouldn't men? We only have to look back a couple of hundred years to see that men used to enjoy dressing up and make-up (albeit this was restricted – as for women – to the wealthy).

Davies (1989) points to the excitement and exhilaration girls can derive from the construction of women as physically strong and heroic. But she and I also demonstrate how this construction is fundamentally at odds with the dominant construction of girls as passive. The hegemonic construction of masculinity as brave, strong, independent and competitive, is also extremely appealing. Wouldn't it be great to be the man who always 'gets' the girl? Indeed, females do appreciate and desire this construction (or else we would not be able to appreciate all the heroes of Western culture and read dominant narratives in the culturally correct manner). Yet according to the dominant construction, females can only get close to this form of masculinity by their involvement in a romantic partnership with such a man, which they achieve when their feminine virtues and beauty are recognised. Likewise, a male's achievement of hegemonic masculinity is what can give him access to the beautiful and (femininely) accomplished woman. The pressures on both genders are terrifying! And as my data shows, children do cross the gender boundaries (as *do* adults). So the challenge for teachers is to show the children how ludicrous are these gender constructions which so profoundly affect our lives and to encourage children to consider crossing the boundaries.

Which tools might dismantle the gender dichotomy?

If we wish to deconstruct gender dichotomy how can we do so? Introducing a few non-sexist books to the classroom, as Davies (1993) has shown, do nothing to *challenge* the gender dichotomy in any way. The trouble is that this dichotomy is something we take for granted in almost every aspect of our lives and have conscious and subconscious desires deeply embedded in it. Children will need more than a few token gestures to set them thinking seriously about it.

Davies (1989) concluded that the gender dichotomy (or 'gender dualism, as she termed it) must be deconstructed to allow children freedom of expression. In her work with Banks (1992, 1993) she embarked on an ambitious programme to teach children about post-structuralism, to enable them to understand the nature of gender discourse and its restrictions on their lives, and to provide them with the tools to deconstruct the gender dichotomy themselves. Her book *Shards of Glass* (1993) describes her endeavours and is illustrated vividly by her own autobiographical writing, but I am not convinced that her pedagogical approach to the gender dichotomy had been very effective. She herself discusses how children found some of the post-structuralist suppositions hard to take on fully and tended to simplify the ideas (for instance thinking in terms of role reversal rather than deconstruction of gender). She also reports coming up against children's powerful desires invested in the gender dichotomy. When I first read about her intention to teach children post-structuralism (Davies and Banks, 1992) I had been sceptical: after all, I was having trouble understanding post-structuralist theory myself, so doubted whether primary school children would comprehend it. I was surprised to find, in *Shards of Glass,* that children had indeed understood some of the most important ideas (albeit in a rather simplified form). However, the post-structuralist theory itself seemed less important than did teaching children about the notion of the oppositional gender dichotomy, how it impacts upon our lives in subtle ways and how unhelpful it is to present the genders as oppositional. Children will not be able to take on the full intricacies of post-structuralism. And if they did there is no guarantee that they would consequently wish to deconstruct the gender dichotomy – there are plenty of non-feminist post-structuralists out there! And it is as feminists that we wish to challenge the gender dichotomy.

Davies' experiments with post-structuralism as a tool for children to challenge dominant gender discourses may have had limited effect. But I support her search for new pedagogical approaches to gender in the classroom. The equal opportunities approaches adopted in the past will inevitably prove inadequate in the face of powerful discourses of gender dichotomy. Anti-sexist teaching is not enough to alter children's constructions of gender fundamentally. The extent to which children used equity discourses in response to my questions initially appears encouraging from a feminist perspective: it shows that such discourses are understood and drawn upon by children, often in order to challenge inequity discourse. However, my data shows many instances where such discourse failed to challenge gender discriminatory constructions.

I also found that while some children attempted to justify and rationalise sexist statements in the knowledge that discriminatory discourse might be rejected by adults in educational environments, they often reasserted their original statements rather than abandon them in the face of my arguments. Their awareness of this discursive clash between equal opportunities and gender discriminatory discourses did not prevent children from articulating gender-discriminatory narratives, even when I undermined their justifications. Though aware of alternative discourses, these children still clung to those which constructed the genders as different. So as Davies and Banks (1992) maintain, equity discourses cannot effectively combat the discursive practice of gender dichotomy. My analysis of gender discourse in the last chapter supports Davies' explanation of this: discourses of equal opportunity do not actually pose a challenge to the construct of genders as relational – upon which sexist discourses are founded.

On analysing the different types of gender-discriminatory discourse I found that all were based upon the hegemonic discourse of gender dichotomy, which children take up in their constructions of gender identity. Equal opportunities discourses are still based on the idea of fixed selves of different genders being given the chance to perform the same activities: the concept of equal opportunities is based on the supposition of difference. Because of this, equal opportunities discourses cannot present any real challenge to the discourse of gender dichotomy, upon which gender-discriminatory discourses, and children's gender constructions, are based. And these constructions might affect children's ability to challenge sexism: we saw in Chapter Four how the construction of the genders as oppositional inhibited effective resistance of sexism, because the assertiveness this required was incongruous with the construction of femininity as sensible and selfless. So for children's constructions of gender as different (and oppositional) to change, a more radical challenge to the discursive gender dichotomy is needed.

My findings suggest that the discourse of 'innate equality between genders' might be one on which teachers could build to challenge the gender dichotomy. There was some evidence of this discourse, like that of equal opportunities, being contained by the dominant discourse of gender duality. But I also found some children using innate equality narratives consistently in their interviews and role-plays, to oppose the construction of genders as different and oppositional. Davies and Banks (1992) argue that discourses which present the genders as equal still fail to challenge the gender dichotomy because children assume their gender identities as part of themselves. Yet I would argue that a discourse which presents the genders as equal in ability at least breaks down the construction of genders as different and therefore appears to have some potential in challenging the gender dichotomy.

How could teachers go about educating children about the gender dichotomy? One suggestion is that teachers and children examine and discuss together reading materials and other information resources[4]. Davies (1989; 1993) suggests that 'alternative' fairy stories and children's books which portray the genders in non-traditional roles can provide new imaginative possibilities for children concerning their gender constructions. (Although, as her book *Frogs and Snails and Feminist Tales* (1989) shows, more thought about child discourses and the aspects of desire embedded in traditional storylines needs to be considered by the authors and purchasers of such books.) Chapter Seven of this book showed that children drew upon resources (TV etc) as evidence to support their preferred gender discourse and frequently rejected counter-stereotypes. So providing children with counter-stereotypical literature and information will not be enough on its own to break down the gender dichotomy.

However, that children *do* draw on resources as evidence in their constructions of gender can be seen as encouraging. Discussion of the gender roles in traditional and non-traditional books and stories can provide a context in which to discuss the gender dichotomy and the oppositional gender constructions it encourages, as well as the ways in which the book characters do or do not conform with such constructions. The teacher could then extend the discussion to constructions of gender in other aspects of life, including the classroom. From my findings about children's responses to the idea of a male childcarer (see Chapter Three) and my speculations about constructions of masculinity and boys' educational 'failure', it seems particularly important that teachers focus on boys' ability to be caring, kind and sensitive as much as girls' ability to be assertive and boisterous.

The idea of discussing gender issues in the primary school classroom has attracted controversy. According to Skelton (1988), teachers can be unwilling to discuss sexism with children because they presume them to be 'innocent'. Short (1988) also found that teachers avoid discussion of 'controversial issues' with children due to their unfounded, Piagetian-based notions that young children have not yet reached the stage of 'formal operations'. My findings suggest that many children are well aware of sexism as an issue and its possible implications for their own lives and future work experiences. A large proportion of girls claimed to experience sexism at the hands of other children, suggesting that Short is right to assert that many teachers underestimate their pupils' level of political understanding. My study demonstrates that a large number of children had an understanding of gender-discrimination and equity issues. The majority of children constructed school as a place where sexism occurs (sometimes against boys as well as girls) and the adult workplace as one of potential gender-discrimination. Although some might worry about the level of cynicism girls displayed about gender equity in the adult world, I suggest that girls' knowledge of this issue and their resentment at its implications could potentially empower them. Awareness of the existence of gender-discrimination as a possible influence on their lives may enable girls to recognise and even challenge it (see Skelton, 1988). Moreover, children's understanding of sexism might encourage them to take a more sympathetic, egalitarian approach to gender issues. So learning about sexism at an early age appears to be advantageous.

Perhaps more problematic is the notion of a teacher persuading children to take a *particular stance* on a controversial issue (ie. the error of constructions of gender as oppositional and of the gender discrimination and power difference resulting from these). Epstein (1993) has discussed this problem in depth in relation to the issue of racism. She argues that if children's expressions of racism are left unchallenged, this in itself legitimates racism. Her argument can be equally applied to sexism. But while it is easy to argue for intervention during sexist incidents, the persuasion of children in a political direction is rather different. Epstein discusses the 'neutral chair' approach, where the (teacher) chair of a discussion maintains a neutral stance. She criticises this approach on grounds that the supposed neutrality is a fallacy and that even very young children are aware of some of their teachers' opinions. Epstein agrees that discussion ought to be open – discriminatory statements from students must be allowed so that they can be discussed and challenged. But they must not be legitimised by the teacher failing to engage with them. She suggests an approach where the teacher tells the children her/his standpoint on the issue at once and then invites children to share their views, adding that there are no right or wrong answers. The different contributions can then be discussed and compared.

Ultimately, if the construction of genders as relational and oppositional is affecting children's freedom of expression and power positions and leading to sexism and discrimination, the issue needs to be tackled positively. A *pro-equality* perspective should be offered to children, which actively attacks discrimination and constructs the genders as *not different*. It is essential that an alternative construction is put forward in place of the traditional gender dichotomy. Educating children about the discursive gender dichotomy from an a-political and a-moral post-structuralist perspective could leave children with no incentive to deconstruct their gender constructions or risk their gender identities. Carrington and Troyna (1988) support egalitarian teaching of 'controversial issues', arguing that it is justified in its encouragement of children to become responsible, thoughtful citizens.

This stance appears justified even within the often restrictive confines of the National Curriculum. Some have argued that the National Curriculum has marginalised topics such as race and gender (see, for instance Hall, 1992). But, as Epstein (1993) notes, many National Curriculum documents contain acknowledgements of the need for equal opportunities. She quotes the National Curriculum Council's *Education for Citizenship* on this component of the curriculum:

> Learning about duties, responsibilities and rights is central to this component. Rights include civil, political, social and human rights and how these may be violated by various forms of injustice, inequality and discrimination, *including sexism and racism*. (NCC, 1990, quoted in Epstein, 1993, her emphasis).

Citizenship remains a 'theme' in cross-curricular elements of the National Curriculum, and although it has been virtually ignored by schools, greater prominance has recently been given to citizenship education by the DfEE and QCA (*The Guardian*, 1998). Teaching about the gender dichotomy and sexism would be an appropriate topic to tackle within the subject of citizenship.

Suggestions for teaching practice

Before I offer practical suggestions for teaching children about oppositional constructions of gender and encouraging children to challenge the gender dichotomy I must point out that as an academic I have not tried out these approaches myself. I draw heavily on the work of people who have tested methods for teaching 'controversial issues' in the primary school, particularly Debbie Epstein (1993) and would welcome feedback from practitioners about the effectiveness of these ideas, and suggestions for new strategies.

According to children's reports, sexist incidents are widespread in primary schools. Teachers must take this behaviour seriously. Epstein (1993) suggests that teachers write down every incidence of racism, to make staff aware how many are taking place and this strategy could be applied to sexist incidents also. Perhaps if children were shown how frequent such incidents were and were made to think about them, they might question such behaviour (on the part of themselves and other children) more readily. Certainly such a technique would demonstrate to children that their behaviour is not to be passed off as 'routine naughtiness' (Skelton, 1997b). Epstein also suggests that such incidents should be seized upon by teachers to provoke discussion. While this seems a useful idea, we know from Davies' (1993) findings that criticism of sexist behaviour will have no effect on its own. Such constructions build upon the dominant discourse of gender dichotomy and cannot be effectively dealt with in isolation, but must be discussed in the context of the gender dichotomy and its impact on our constructions of gender.

Accordingly, I have suggested that teachers draw on the discourse of innate equality between genders to provoke discussion (and to maintain as a position within discussion). As noted at the beginning of this book, children will draw on physical differences between the sexes to illustrate gender difference. It will be the teachers' task to show children how superficial these physical differences are; that the vast difference between our society's constructions of the two genders is hugely disproportionate to any physical differences; and how diverse human beings are physically. So if, for example, children point out that male athletes run faster than women athletes, teachers could respond that current female athletes run faster than male athletes did twenty years ago and that they can run faster than most non-athlete men. It is the *diversity* of physical difference which needs to be stressed (some women are bigger and stronger than some men, some men are more agile than some women), perhaps helped by resources (pictures of women body builders etc).

The ways in which skills are attributed to different genders in different societies or points in history can also be used to show the random nature of apparent gender differences. We have seen how skills such as weaving were ascribed to males in some parts of the world and females in others, and how it is ascribed higher social status in the countries where it is practised by men. Cohen (1993) provides another example: during the centuries when speaking French was both fashionable and necessary for the upper classes in Britain, it was argued that women were inept at learning the language and men were far superior at learning foreign languages. Yet now that French has lower status as a subject in schools, girls vastly out-perform boys in achievement and are often assumed to be 'naturally' better at languages. The aspect to stress is the *similarity* between men and women. Examples of women and men performing non-traditional roles and jobs and discussion of men's and women's similar feelings and achievements could be used to illustrate this point. Discussion could then move to ideas about gender constructions which cause girls/women and boys/men to behave so differently and perform different roles in society. I suggest three areas for the bases of this discussion: children's books and media resources, the classroom, and adult work.

Returning to discussing the characters and gender constructions in children's books, an engaging and stimulating method of raising this issue with children which, as Epstein (1993) points out, also provides valuable reading practice. Wing (1997) describes using *Bill's New Frock* by Anne Fine in this way. Its likeable protagonist, Bill, wakes up one morning to find he has become a girl. The book's sympathetic and humorous portrayal of the subsequent difference in attitude he en-counters in his various interactions at school provoked intense interest and amusement amongst the children. Wing maintains that the book challenged children's gender assumptions and helped girls and boys articulate their complaints about gender constructions in the sub-sequent discussion. They were politicised by this articulation and appeared to benefit by being forced to consider school life 'in the other gender's shoes'. Other books Davies (1989) recommends are *The Paper Bag Princess* and *Rosie the Rescuer*, although teachers should be warned that Davies found certain child discourses about 'messiness' impacting on children's interpretation of the former book; and that boys tended not to engage with Rosie's girlhood in the latter. Both Wing and Davies show how important it is for teachers to discuss these storylines with children so they can make the most of the issues raised. Equally importantly they show how much fascination and enjoyment children showed in reading or being read such stories.

After discussing gender constructions in the context of such books which actively question and challenge traditional gender positions, more traditional books and fairy stories can be explored, and possibly television programmes (which my research shows children hugely enjoy discussing). The gender constructions within these texts can be questioned in general discussion. Epstein (1993) suggests that children be given tasks, such as inventing new story endings or alternative plots for these traditional texts and writing book reviews examining their level of gender stereotypical content. These techniques also help children develop their writing and reading skills.

Once the notion of the gender dichotomy, ideas (discourses) emanating from it and subsequent dominant gender constructions have been discussed with children, attention can be paid to how these constructions are manifesting themselves during classroom interaction. Obviously it is important that names not be named here – children should not feel personally criticised or under examination. But general constructions of masculinity and femininity in class and school can be discussed, showing children how restrictive and nonsensical they are.

The genders of people performing various jobs in the school could also be talked about and this discussion extended to adult occupations in general. My work has shown that many children are aware of equal opportunities discourse in this area and that adult occupation is a topic which engages them. As well as developing their knowledge of adult occupation and notions of equality, teachers might also provoke children to question why women and men are clustered in different areas of adult work and why (for the moment at least) men hold the most powerful occupational positions in our society. However, this requires careful discussion with reference to the gender dichotomy, otherwise drawing attention to traditional roles might reinforce rather than challenge children's stereotypical constructions of gender.

During these discussions, Davies (1993) argues, children need to come to see themselves both as producers and consumers of culture. And the intention – the *deconstruction* of the dichotomous notion of gender dichotomy – should not be lost sight of. Children must not be allowed to think that the teacher is simply suggesting role reversals. Because gender constructions are part of identity and also such a contentious issue, the discussions may become heated. It will be up to the teachers to make sure that neither the boys nor the girls feel marginalised or silenced. Epstein (1993) also makes the important point that children should not be pressurised or forced to speak. She is writing about race but it would be easy to suppose that both boys and girls could feel uncomfortable about discussions of this nature, for a variety of reasons. They might be wary of risking their carefully maintained gender construction, or the boys might feel threatened or defensive when gender discrimination and sexism in the classroom are discussed. It must also be remembered that the dominant construction of gender is not the only one: not all children are heterosexual and this book shows how many children are already constructing themselves in alternative ways. Such children must not be made to feel more 'different' through discussions of gender issues. However, the findings of Davies (1993) and Wing (1997) from similar work with mixed sex groups suggests that the majority of children relish the chance for such debate. Finally, teachers should not feel bad if they initially find themselves occasionally slipping into the terminology or discourse of gender dichotomy. While this is obviously to be avoided if possible, Davies' experiences show that such slips are almost inevitable. The main thing is to learn from them.

Although the discussion of gender in these contexts may not lead to immediate, dramatic change in children's oppositional gender constructions, it might serve to stem the excesses of gender category maintenance (such as sexist incidents) and to empower children intellectually to challenge them. It will enable them to challenge constructions and assumptions emanating from the dominant discourse of gender dichotomy if they wish. Moreover, it will provide children with extra information, fantasies and discursive resources which they can draw on to create more flexible constructions of their own gender identity if they want to.

Notes

1) See Gaskell (1992) and also Spender (1982)

2) See the work of Stanworth (1981), Clarricoates (1980) and Skelton (1997).

3) Feminists have written extensively on the pressure on women to diet and to conform to a particular image of beauty (Orbach, 1989). A good collection is Chapkiss' *Beauty Secrets* (1988). There is also a large body of work on the narratives of romance and the appeal they hold for women and girls (see, for example, Dowling, 1981; McRobbie, 1978; Walkerdine, 1997).

4) Wing (1997) has suggested that the examination and discussion of children's books and stories helps children to recognise and question gender stereotypes. Davies (1993) and Gonick (1997) present books and magazines as useful resources which can provide the bases of discussion, as well as information and fantasy about new, alternative gender positions children could adopt.

APPENDIX 1

INTERVIEW QUESTIONS

1) Why did you chose that role in the play?

2) How did you think you acted?

3) Did you think everyone chose the right parts, and acted them well?

4) What about the work problem? Was it solved realistically?

5) Is the job you took in the play something you would like to do in real life?

6) What job would you like to do when you leave school?

7) Do your parents know you want to do that job? If so, do they approve?

8) Is the job you've chosen the same as your parents'?

9) Can a woman/man do the job you have chosen?

10) Do men and women have the ability to do all jobs? (and if not, why not?)

11) Are men or women better at certain jobs? (and if so, why?)

12) Would you use the service of a female builder/female lorry driver/male childcarer?

13) How would male builders treat a new female builder?

14) How would the same male builders react to a woman boss?

15) Would a boss prefer men to do some jobs and women others, or would they have both sexes doing all jobs?

16) Do girls and boys behave differently in class or not? (if so, in what way?)

17) Are girls and boys just acting differently, or are they really different inside?

18) Do you know what the word 'sexism' means?

19) In class, do boys ever pick on girls just because they're girls, or girls pick on boys just because they're boys?

REFERENCES

Abrams, J. (1996) Postitivism, Prejudice and Progress in the Sociology of Education: who's afraid of values?, *British Journal of Sociology of Education*, 17 (1) pp. 81-86

Adams, C. and Walkerine, V. (1986) *Investigating Gender in the Primary School*, London: Inner London Eeducation Authority

Arnot, M. (1997) Gendered Citizenry: new feminist perspectives on education and citizenship, *British Educational Research Journal*, 23 (3) pp. 275-295

Bailey, M. (1993) Foucauldian Feminism: contesting bodies, sexuality and identity, in Ramazanoglu, C. (ed) *Up Against Foucault*, London: Routledge

Baker, C. and Davies, B. (1989) A Lesson on Sex Roles, *Gender and Education*, 1 (1) pp. 59-75

Balbus, I. (1987) Disciplining Women: Michel Foucault and the power of feminist discourse, in Benhabib, S. and Cornell, D. (eds.) *Feminism as Critique*, London: Polity Press

Barthes, R. (1973) S/Z, Paris: Editions du Seuil

Barthes, R. (1990) *The Pleasure of the Text*, Oxford: Basil Blackwell

Belotti, E. (1975) *Little Girls*, London: Writers and Readers Publishing Co-op

Bennet, B. (1991) The Promotion of Dance in Secondary Schools, unpublished MPhil, Leicester: Leicester Polytechnic

Berti, A. and Bombi, A. (1988) *The Child's Construction of Economics*, Cambridge: Cambridge University Press

Billig, M. (1987) *Arguing and Thinking*, Cambridge: Cambridge University Press

Billig, M. *et al,* (1988) *Ideological Dilemmas*, London: Sage

Billig, M. (1992) *Talking of the Royal Family*, London: Routledge

Blyth, A. (1992) Themes and Dimensions: Icing or Spicing? In Hall, G (ed.) *Themes and Dimensions of the National Curriculum*, London: Kogan Page

Bordo, S. (1990) Feminism, Postmodernism and Gender Scepticism, in Nicholson, L. (ed.) *Feminism/Postmodernism*, London: Routledge

Buckingham, D. (1993) *Children Talking Television*, Lewes: Falmer Press

Carrington, B. And Troyna, B. (1988) Combating Racism through Political Education, in Carrington, B. And Troyna, B. *Children and Controvsersial Issues*, Lewes: Falmer Press

Central Statistical Office, (1995) *Social Focus on Women,* London: The Stationery Office

Centre for Contemporary Cultural Studies, (1982) T*he Empire Strikes Back,* London: Hutchinson

Chapkiss, W. (1988) *Beauty Secrets,* London: The Women's Press

Clarricoates, K. (1980) The Importance of Being Ernest... Emma... Tom... Jane, in Deem, R. (ed.) *Schooling for Women's Work,* London: Routledge and Kegan Paul

Cockburn, C. (1987) *Two Track Training,* London: Macmillan Education

Cockburn, C. (1991) *In the Way of Women,* London: Macmillan

Cohen, M. (1993) A Genealogy of Conversation: Gender Subjectivation and Learning French in England, unpublished Ph.D, London: Institute of Education, University of London

Cole, M. and Hill, D. (1995) Games of Despair and Rhetorics of Resistance: postmodernism, education and reaction, in *British Journal of Sociology of Education,* 16 (2) pp.165-182

Connell, R. (1987) *Gender and Power,* Cambridge: Polity Press

Connell, R. (1995) *Masculinities,* Cambridge: Polity Press

Connor, S. (1993) The Necessity of Value, in Squires, J. (ed.) *Principled Positions: Postmodernism and the Rediscovery of Value,* London: Lawrence and Wishart

Cullingford, C. and Brown, G. (1995) Children's Perceptions of Victims and Bullies, *Education 3-13,* 23 (2) pp.11-16

Damon, W. (1977) *The Social World of the Child,* San Francisco: Jossey-Bass

Davies, B. (1989) *Frogs and Snails and Feminist Tales,* Sydney: Allen and Unwin

Davies, B. (1993) *Shards of Glass,* Sydney: Allen and Unwin

Davies, B. and Banks, C. (1992) The Gender Trap: a feminist-poststructuralist analysis of primary school children's talk about gender, *Junior Curriculum Studies,* 24 (1) pp. 1-25

Davis, K. (1988) *Power Under the Microscope,* Dordrecht: Foris Publications

Delamont, S. (1980) *Sex Roles and the School,* London: Methuen

Denscombe, M. (1995) Explorations in Group Interviews: an evaluation of a reflexive and partisan approach, *British Educational Research Journal,* 21 (2) pp.131- 138

Derrida, J. (1966) Structure, Sign and Play in the Discourse of the Human Sciences, in Derrida, J. (ed.) *Writing and Difference,* Chicago: University of Chicago Press

Derrida, J. (1976) *Of Grammatology,* Baltimore: John Hopkins University Press

Dixon, B. (1990) *Playing Them False,* Stoke-on-Trent: Trentham Books

Dowling, C. (1982) *The Cinderella Complex,* London: Fontana

Durkin, K. (1985) *Television, Sex Roles, and Children,* Milton Keynes: Open University Press

Edley and Wetherell (1995) *Men in Perspective*, Hemel Hempstead: Prentice Hall and Harvester Wheatsheaf

Epstein, D. (1993) *Changing Classroom Cultures*, Stoke-on-Trent: Trentham Books

Equal Opportunities Commission Report, (1996) *Educational Reforms and Gender Equality in Schools*, Manchester: Equal Opportunities Commission

Equal Opportunities Commission, (1997) *Briefings on Women and Men in Britain*, Manchester: Equal Opportunities Commission

Foucault, M. (1967) *Madness and Civilisation*, London: Tavistock

Foucault, M. (1972) *The Archaeology of Knowledge*, London: Tavistock

Foucault, M. (1977) *Discipline and Punish: The Birth of the Prison*, London: Tavistock

Foucault, M. (1980) *Power/Knowledge: Selected Interviews and Other Writings, 1972-1977*, New York: Pantheon

Foucault, M. (1981) *The History of Sexuality: Volume 1: An Introduction*, Harmondsworth: Penguin

Francis, B. (1998a) Oppositional Positions: children's construction of gender in talk and role-plays based on adult occupation, Educational Research, 40 (1) pp. 31-43

Francis, B. (1998b: forthcoming) An Investigation of the Discourses Children Draw on in their Constructions of Gender, *Journal of Applied Social Psychology*

Fraser, N. and Nicholson, L. (1990) Social Criticism Without Philosophy: an encounter between feminism and postmodernism, in Nicholson, L. (ed.) *Feminism/ Postmodernism*, London: Routledge

Frueh, T. and Mcghee, P. (1975) Traditional Sex-Role Development, and Amount of Time Spent Watching Television, *Developmental Psychology*, 11 pp. 109- 110

Gaskell, J. (1992) *Gender Matters From School to Work*, Buckingham: Open University Press

Gonick, M. (1997) Reading Selves, Re-fashioning Identity: teen magazines and their readers, *Curriculum Studies*, 5 (1) pp. 69-86

Grabrucker, M. (1988) There's a Good Girl, London: The Women's Press

Griffiths, M. (1995) Making a Difference: feminism, post-modernism and the methodology of educational research, *British Educational Research Journal*, 21 (2) pp. 219-236

The Guardian, 15/5/98

Gunter, B. and Mcaleer, J. (1990) *Children and Television: The One Eyed Monster*, London: Routledge

Hall, G. (1992) Does the Curriculum Match the Reality? In HALL, G. (Ed) *Themes and Dimensions of the National Curriculum*, London: Kogan Page

Harding, S. (1984) Is Gender a Variable in Conceptions of Rationality? in Gould, C. (ed.) *Beyond Domination*, London: Rowman and Allenheld

Harding, S. (1990) Feminism, Science, and the Anti-Enlightenment Critiques, in Nicholson, L. (ed.) *Feminism/Postmodernism*, London: Routledge

Harding, S. (1991) *Whose Science? Whose Knowledge?* Buckingham: Open University Press

Hartsock, N. (1990) Foucault on Power: a Theory for Women, in Nicholson, L. (ed.) *Feminism/Postmodernism*, London: Routledge

Haworth, J. *et al*, (1992) Home Sweet Home Corner, *Education 3-13*, 20 (1) pp. 37-42

Hearn, J. and MOrgan, D. (1995) Contested Discourses on Men and Masculinities, in Blair, M. Holland, J. and Sheldon, S. (eds.) *Identity and Diversity: Gender and the Experience of Education*, Buckingham: Open University Press

Herbert, C. (1989) *Talking of Silence – The Sexual Harassment of Schoolgirls*, London: Falmer

Hey, V. (1997) *The Company She Keeps,* Buckingham: Open University Press

Holland, J. and Skouras, G. (1979) Study of Adolescent's Views of Aspects of the Social Division of Labour, *Sociological Research Unit/Social Science Research Council Report*, No. 6

hooks, b. (1982) *Ain't I a Woman?* London: Pluto

hooks, b (1989) *Talking Back: Thinking Feminist, Thinking Black*, London: Sheba

Hutchings, M. (1990) Children's Thinking About Work, in Ross, A. (ed.) *Economic and Industrial Awareness in the Primary School*, London: PNL Press

Hutchings, M. (1995) Children's Ideas About Payment for Work, *Economic Awareness*, 7 (2) pp. 28-34

Jones, A. (1993) Becoming a 'Girl': post-structuralist suggestions for educational research, *Gender and Education*, 5 (2) pp. 157-166

Jones, A. (1997) Teaching Post-structuralist Feminist Theory in Education: student resistances, *Gender and Education*, 9 (3) pp. 261-269

Jordan, E. (1995) Fighting Boys and Fantasy Play: the construction of masculinity in the early years of school, *Gender and Education*, 7 (1) pp. 69-86

Kelly, A. (1989) 'When I Grow Up I Want to Be...': a longitudinal study of the development of career preferences, *British Journal of Guidance and Counselling*, 17 (2) pp. 179-200

Kenway, J. et al (1994) Making 'Hope Practical' Rather Than 'Despair Convincing': feminist poststructuralism, gender reform and educational change, *British Journal of Sociology of Education*, 15 (2) pp. 187-210

Kohlberg, L. (1966) A Cognitive Developmental Analysis of Children's Sex-role Concepts and Attitudes, in Maccoby, E. (ed.) *Development of Sex Differences*, Stanford, CA: Stanford University Press

Larkin, J. (1994) Walking Through Walls: the sexual harassment of highschool girls, *Gender and Education*, 6 (3) pp. 263-280

Lave, J. and Wenger, E. (1991) *Situated Learning*, Cambridge: Cambridge University Press

Lees, S. (1993) *Sugar and Spice*, Harmondsworth: Penguin

Lightbody, P. et al (1996) Motivation and Attribution at Secondary School: the role of gender, *Educational Studies*, 2 (1) pp. 13-25

Lightbody, P. and Durndell, A. (1996) Gendered Career Choice: is sex-stereotyping the cause or the consequence? *Educational Studies*, 2 (2) pp. 133-146

Lindholm, L. (1978) *Pupils' Attitudes to Equality Between the Sexes*, Malmo: CWK Gleerup

Lloyd, B. and Duveen, G. (1992) *Gender Identities and Education*, London: Harvester Wheatsheaf

Lyotard, F. (1984) *The Post-Modern Condition*, Manchester: Manchester University Press

Mac an Ghaill, M. (1994) *The Making of Men*, Buckingham: Open University Press

Macnaghten, P. (1993) Discourses of Nature: Argumentation and Power, in Burman, E. and Parker, I. (eds.) *Discourse Analytical Research*, London: Routledge

Marshall, A. (1994) Sensuous Sapphires: A Study of the Social Construction of Black Female Sexuality, in Maynard, M. and Purvis, P. (eds.) *Researching Women's Lives From a Feminist Perspective*, London: Taylor and Francis

Maynard, M. (1994) Methods, Practice and Epistemology: The Debate About Feminism and Research, in Maynard, M. and Purvis, J. (eds.) *Researching Women's Lives From a Feminist Perspective*, London: Taylor and Francis

Maynard, M. and Purvis, J. (eds.) (1994) *Researching Women's Lives From a Feminist Perspective*, London: Taylor and Francis

Mcrobbie, A. (1978) *Jackie: An Ideology of Adolescent Femininity*, Birmingham: Centre for Contemporary Cultural Studies

Middleton, P. (1992) *The Inward Gaze: Masculinity and Subjectivity in Modern Culture*, London: Routledge

National Curriculum Council (1990) *Curriculum Guidance 8*. Education for Citizenship, York: NCC

Nemerowicz, G. (1979) *Children's Perceptions of Gender and Work Roles*, New York: Praegar Publishers

Nilan, P. (1995) Negotiating Gendered Identity in Classroom Disputes and Collaboration, *Discourse and Society*, 6 (1) pp. 27-47

Orbach, S. (1989) *Fat is a Feminist Issue*, London: Arrow

Pattinson, T. (1991) *Sexual Harassment: The Hidden Facts*, London: Futura

Phoenix, A. (1987) Theories of Gender and Black Families, in Weiner, G. and Arnot, M. (eds.) *Gender Under Scrutiny*, Milton Keynes: Open University Press

Phoenix, A. (1994) Practicing Research: The Intersection of Gender and 'Race' in the Research Process, in Maynard, M. and Purvis, J. (eds.) *Researching Women's Lives From a Feminist Perspective*, London: Taylor and Francis

Piaget, J. (1964) *Six Psychological Studies*, (ed. Elkind, D.) Geneve, S.A: Editions Gonthier

Potter, J. and Wetherell, M. (1987) *Discourse and Social Psychology: Beyond Attitudes and Behaviour,* London: Sage

Ramazanoglu, C. (ed.) (1993) *Up Against Foucault,* London: Routledge

Reay, D. (1990) Girls' Groups as a Component of Anti-sexist Practice; one primary school's experience, *Gender and Education,* 2 (1) pp. 37- 47

Riddell, S. (1989) Pupils, Resistance and Gender Codes, *Gender and Education,* 1 (2) pp. 183-196

Robb, B. (1981) Maternal Employment and Children's Sex Role Perceptions, *Educational Research,* 23 (3) pp. 223-225

Rose, N. (1989) Individualising Psychology, in Shotter, J. and Gergen, K. (eds.) *Texts of Identity,* London: Sage

Rosenthal, D. and Chapman, D. (1982) The Lady Spaceman: children's perceptions of sex-stereotyped occupations, *Sex Roles,* 8 (9) pp. 959-965

Ross, A. (1990) Children's Perceptions of Industrial Hierarchies, in Ross, A. (ed.) *Economic and Industrial Awareness in the Primary School,* London: PNL Press

Ross, A. (1992) Children's Perceptions of Capital, in Hutchings, M. and Wade, W. (eds.) *Developing Economic and Industrial Understanding in the Primary School,* London: PNL Press

Sarah, E. (1980) Teachers and Students in the classroom: an examination of classroom interaction, in Spender, D. and Sarah, E. (eds.) *Learning to Lose: Sexism and Education,* London: The Women's Press

Sarbin, T. (1986) (ed.) *Narrative Psychology: The Storied Nature of Human Conduct,* New York: Praegar

Sassure, F. (1916) *Course in General Linguistics,* Trans. Wade, B. (159) London: Fontana

Sealey, A. and Knight, C. (1990) 'We Don't Like Talking in Front of the Boys': talk and inequality, *Education 3-13,* 18 (3) pp. 55-59

Sharpe, S. (1976) *Just Like a Girl,* Harmondsworth: Penguin

Short, G. (1988) Children's Grasp of Controversial Issues, in Carrington, B. and Troyna, B. (eds.) *Children and Controversial Issues,* Lewes: Falmer

Short, G. (1993) Sex-typed Behaviour in the Primary School: the significance of contrasting expectations, *Educational Research,* 35 (1) pp. 77-87

Short, G. and Carrington, B. (1989) Discourse on Gender: the perceptions of children aged between six and eleven, in Skelton, C. (ed.) *Whatever Happens to Little Women? Gender and Primary Schooling,* Milton Keynes: Open University Press

Shotter, J. (1989) Social Accountability and the Social Construction of 'You', in Shotter, J. and Gergen, K. (eds.) *Texts of Identity,* London: Sage Publications

Shotter, J. (1993) *Cultural Politics of Everyday Life,* Buckingham: Open University Press

Silverman, D. (1993) *Interpreting Qualitative Data,* London: Sage

Skeggs, B. (1994) Situating the Production of Feminist Methodology, in Maynard, M. and Purvis, J. (eds.) *Researching Women's Lives From a Feminist Perspective*, London: Taylor and Francis

Skelton, C. (1988) Demolishing 'The House That Jack Built': anti-sexist initiatives in the primary school classroom, in Carrington, B. and Troyna, B. (eds.) *Children and Controversial Issues*, London: Falmer

Skelton, C. (1997a) Girls and hegemonic masculinity in the primary school, presented at BERA conference, University of York, 11-14 September

Skelton, C. (1997b) Primary Boys and Hegemonic Masculinities, *British Journal of Sociology of Education*, 18 (3) pp. 349-368

Smithers, A. (1984) An Exploratory Study of Sex Role Differentiation Among Young Children, *Educational Review*, 36 (1) pp. 87-99

Soper, K. (1990) *Troubled Pleasures*, London: Verso

Soper, K. (1993a) Productive Contradictions, in Ramazanoglu, C. (ed.) Up *Against Foucault*, London: Routledge

Soper, K. (1993b) Postmodernism, Subjectivity and the Question of Value, in Squires, J. (ed.) *Principled Positions: Postmodernism and the Rediscovery of Value*, London: Routledge

Spender, D. (1980) Education or Indoctrination?, in Spender, D. and Sarah, E. (eds.) *Learning to Lose: Sexism and Education*, London: The Women's Press

Spender, D. (1982) *Invisible Women: The Schooling Scandal*, London: Writers and Readers

Spretnak, C. (1993) *States of Grace*, London: Harper Collins

Squires, J. (1993) Introduction, in Squires, (ed.) *Principled Positions: Postmodernism and the Rediscovery of Value*, London: Lawrence and Wishart

Stafford, A. (1991) *Trying Work: Gender, Youth and Work Experience*, Edinburgh: Edinburgh University Press

STANLEY, L. and Wise, S. (1993) *Breaking Out Again: Feminist Ontology and Epistemology*, London: Routledge

Stanworth, M. (1981) *Gender and Schooling*, London: Hutchinson

Steedman, C. (1982) *The Tidy House*, London: Virago

Taylor, M. (1986) Pupils' Attitudes Towards Gender Roles, *Educational Research*, 28 (3) pp. 202-209

Tett, L. (1997) Changing Masculinities? Single-sex work with boys and young men, *Youth and Policy*, 55, pp. 14-27

Thomas, K. (1990) *Gender and Subject in Higher Education*, Buckingham: Open University Press

Thorne, B. (1993) *Gender Play: Girls and Boys in School*, Buckingham: Open University Press

Times Educational Supplement (29/11/1995)

Tremaine, L. (1982) Children's Occupational Sex-Typing, *Sex Roles*, 8 (7) pp. 691-710

Troyna, B. and Hatcher, R. (1992) *Racism in Children's Lives*, London: Routledge

Vicks, H. (1990) The Use of Drama in an Anti-Sexist Classroom, in Tutchell, E. (ed.) *Dolls and Dungarees*, Milton Keynes: Open University Press

Walkerdine, V. (1981) Sex, Power and Pedagogy, *Screen Education*, 38, pp. 14-21

Walkerdine, V. (1988) *The Mastery of Reason*, London: Routledge

Walkerdine, V. *et al*, (1989) *Counting Girls Out*, London: Virago

Walkerdine, V. (1990) *Schoolgirl Fictions*, London: Verso

Walkerdine, V. (1997) *Daddy's Girl*, Basingstoke: MacMillan Press

Walkerdine, V. and Lucey, H. (1989) *Democracy in the Kitchen*, London:Virago

Weedon, C. (1987) *Feminist Practice and Poststructuralist Theory*, Oxford: Basil Blackwell

Weiner, G. et al (1997) Educational Reform, Gender and Class in Britain: epistemological and methodological questions, paper presented at the ECER conference, Frankfurt

Whitehead, J. (1996) Sex Stereotypes, Gender Identity and Subject Choice at A-Level, *Educational Research*, 38 (2) pp. 147-160

Whitney, I. and Smith, P. (1993) A Survey of the Nature and Extent of Bullying in Junior/Middle and Secondary Schools, *Educational Research*, 35 (1) pp. 3-25

Whyte, J. (1986) *Beyond the Wendy House: Sex Role Stereotyping in Primary Schools*, York: Longman

Willis, P. (1977) *Learning to Labour*, London: Saxon House

Wing, A. (1997) How Can Children Be Taught to Read Differently? Bill's New Frock and the 'Hidden Curriculum', *Gender and Education*, 9 (4) pp.491-504

Yates, L. (1997) Gender Equity and the Boys Debate: what sort of challenge is it? *British Journal of Sociology of Education*, 18 (3) pp. 337-348

Index

KING ALFRED'S COLLEGE
LIBRARY

1259